POWER
OF 5
INVESTING®

# — 5 —
# POWERFUL
# PRINCIPLES

FOR RETIREMENT INVESTING

ERIK J. CHRISTMAN, CFP®, CPA

*Advantage*®

Published by Advantage, Charleston, South Carolina. Member of Advantage Media Group.

ADVANTAGE is a registered trademark and the Advantage colophon is a trademark of Advantage Media Group, Inc.

POWER OF 5 INVESTING is a registered trademark of Siena Capital, LLC d/b/a Oxford Financial Partners.

Printed in the United States of America.
ISBN: 978-1-59932-538-5
LCCN: 2015942303

This publication is designed to provide accurate and authoritative information in regard to the subject matter covered. It is sold with the understanding that the publisher is not engaged in rendering legal, accounting, or other professional services. If legal advice or other expert assistance is required, the services of a competent professional person should be sought.

Advantage Media Group is proud to be a part of the Tree Neutral® program. Tree Neutral offsets the number of trees consumed in the production and printing of this book by taking proactive steps such as planting trees in direct proportion to the number of trees used to print books. To learn more about Tree Neutral, please visit www.treeneutral.com. To learn more about Advantage's commitment to being a responsible steward of the environment, please visit www.advantagefamily.com/green

Advantage Media Group is a publisher of business, self-improvement, and professional development books and online learning. We help entrepreneurs, business leaders, and professionals share their Stories, Passion, and Knowledge to help others Learn & Grow. Do you have a manuscript or book idea that you would like us to consider for publishing? Please visit advantagefamily.com or call 1.866.775.1696.

*To Phil and Judy,*
*for making me who I am.*


*To Holli,*
*for making me better than I ever dreamed I could be.*


*To Jackson and Kaitlyn,*
*for all that I know you will become.*

# ABOUT THE AUTHOR

**Erik J. Christman, CFP®, CPA**
**Managing Partner**
erik@oxfordfp.com

Erik is managing partner of Oxford Financial Partners, a premier fee-based wealth management firm. As managing partner, Erik is responsible for the strategic direction and future growth of the firm. Erik leads a team of talented individuals at Oxford and leverages their expertise in portfolio design, retirement income distribution, estate planning, and tax reduction strategies to design innovative solutions for current and prospective clients.

Erik is the creator of *Power of 5 Investing*®, a unique system for helping clients achieve retirement success. He has appeared in national publications including *Money* and *Forbes* and has been listed as a Five Star Wealth Advisor multiple times in *Cincinnati Magazine*.

Erik is a CERTIFIED FINANCIAL PLANNER® professional, Certified Public Accountant (CPA), a FINRA Series 7 Registered Representative, a FINRA Series 24 Registered Principal, an Investment Advisor Representative, and is insurance licensed. He received his MBA in finance from Indiana University and completed his undergraduate studies at Miami University with dual majors in finance and accountancy. His two decades of professional experience has included key roles for leading companies including Procter &

Gamble, Deloitte & Touche, and the Western & Southern Financial Group. He is a past president of the Financial Planning Association of Greater Cincinnati and has served on the local board of the Miami University Alumni Association. Erik was selected to the prestigious C-Change program sponsored by the Cincinnati USA Regional Chamber, a program dedicated to improving the image and quality of life in Cincinnati.

Erik and his wife Holli live in Greenwood Village, Colorado, with their two children, a rescue dog, and a mixed breed dog and are members of Colorado Community Church in Denver. Holli's career includes nearly 20 years in marketing and brand management with Procter & Gamble, and she continues with her own marketing and strategy consulting firm today. In his spare time, Erik enjoys all that the Colorado outdoors has to offer and is an avid fan of his children's many athletic and artistic pursuits.

# TABLE OF CONTENTS

# PREFACE

## BUILDING FROM A STRONG FOUNDATION

I was adopted when I was three months old. In their announcement of my arrival, my parents wrote that I wasn't expected, I was selected. Growing up, it was clear to me that they wanted me more than anything in the world, and they gave their utmost to provide a good family life. I knew they had my back—and that I had their love and support, come what may. We even weathered my period of teenage surliness.

While some children grow up fearing failure, I never felt that—and it was because of the support and encouragement my parents gave me. I always felt that we could make things work out and that we should learn from the past but aim for a better future. I have come to recognize that among the many things my parents did well, helping me stay focused on my future no matter what challenges came my way, stands out. Both were from traditional German families and had the stubborn and doggedly determined characteristics of their heritage.

I will never forget the phone call from my father one day in 1989 when I was at my dormitory at Miami University in Ohio. He told me that my mother had breast cancer. Never one to quit, she would fight bravely for several years until a relapse took her in 1997, when I was still in my 20s.

By the time of her diagnosis, the dominoes already were falling at the bank where my father was the chief operating officer. A merger he helped engineer with a larger bank would eventually lead to his being unceremoniously dumped. He had worked for years to advance his career and build a comfortable retirement with the only woman he had ever loved. Instead, he found himself an unemployed widower at the young age of 55. My father's years of toil had taken a toll on his health as well—diabetes and congestive heart failure—and he went on permanent disability the year after my mother passed. He died about seven years later, in early 2005.

My parents died way too young—she was 55, he was 62. Losing them was incredibly painful and remains the most difficult period of my life. But that early experience instilled in me sensitivity to the issues that people face as they get older, and it helped to prepare me for a career that, at the time, I'd never imagined I would pursue.

## LESSONS FOR A LIFETIME

Despite the hardships, my parents packed a tremendous amount of life and love into the time they had. Through them, I developed empathy for people as they approach and go through their retirement years—an understanding that has served me well as a financial advisor who specializes in such matters. It was not the loss of my parents, however, that made me a better financial advisor. It was what I gained from them.

I've been told—more than once—that I am highly confident, which can also come across as intimidating or even cocky (and I've certainly been called worse). But I think the reason I come across as confident is that I know who I am and what I believe in. A lot of that came from my upbringing.

When I think about the lessons my parents taught me, I realize that they have become the foundations by which I live my life overall. And those foundations impact my relationships not only with my family and friends but also my employees and my clients. You'll see whispers of these foundations as you read the rest of the book.

Surround yourself with people who love and understand you. And then realize that it's okay if some other people *don't* like you. My parents had a very tight circle of family and friends and cared passionately about them. The people who mattered the most to them *really* mattered. They would do anything for them. And they really didn't care what anybody else thought. It's not that they were flippant or cruel or oblivious. They just knew what—and who—mattered and focused on that. They knew their personalities and approach to life would not be for everyone. And they were okay with that.

As a preacher of mine once said, "We spend an inordinate amount of time wondering what people who we don't even like think about us." It's true. Lots of time and energy can be spent thinking about what everyone else around you thinks about your opinions, your clothes, your politics, or your hair. At the end of the day, the only people who matter are those who you choose to make a part of your life.

Today, I surround myself with quality people who tell me the truth about myself. I have a staff that respects and likes me and vice versa. My wife has no problem telling me what she thinks. And she will tell you that I am not a people pleaser. I lay it on the table, and you can choose if it works for you or not. If you don't buy in to me or my approach, that's okay. I'm okay if everyone doesn't hire me. It's probably for the best sometimes. And I'm okay if everyone doesn't like me. That's probably for the best, too.

There *are* some things that are black and white. Boy, did my parents have strong opinions about the way things should be. Sometimes embarrassingly so; I vividly recall a trip to Italy when my father could have been the poster child for the ugly American when he repeatedly insisted that he *must* have ice in his drinks (among other mortifying moments). They just wouldn't budge on their point of view for some specific things.

For me, there are some things where I don't buy the shades of gray mentality. There are just some things that *are*. Don't hit women or children. Don't cheat to get ahead. Be honest and transparent about what's in front of you. Find a plan and stick with it. I like people who have opinions and are true to who they are. And I like to ensure that my clients know exactly what they're buying and who I am when they hire me.

*The age-old traits of authenticity, honesty, and consistency matter.* Even when my dad went through a tragic shift in his career, he remained as dedicated and focused as ever. My mother was also honest, maybe even to a fault. I always knew what to expect of them—whether they were punishing me for something they'd already told me not to do, rewarding me for an accomplishment, or telling me how they were going to face their latest health or life challenge.

I don't sugarcoat things—not with my children (who will tell you I am sometimes *too* honest in my criticism), not with my wife, and not with my clients. In this profession, you should know what to expect of me, and I of you. I will never tell a client their financial future looks secure if it doesn't or that I think they're making a sound decision if I don't. Sometimes it's hard to say it—and sometimes it's certainly not what they want to hear. But you can only make good decisions if you know what you're dealing with. It's my job to be honest and consistent in the face of all the other moving parts. I do that in my life, and I do it in my practice.

And—most importantly—life is too short to be unhappy, worried, and pessimistic. Grab it by the proverbial horns, and go for it. My parents were extraordinarily good at this. They loved life. They loved having fun. They loved each other and me and their family and friends. They took me to fancy restaurants at a way too young age. They traveled. They spent money on the things that mattered to them. They partied and laughed and created memories every chance they got. They worried very little. I don't think they had very many regrets. What an awesome way to live—and frankly, to die. And while I will never get over being angry and sad that they were gone too soon, I will also never stop admiring them for how they lived and what they got out of the too-few years that they had. If they taught me one big lesson, this was it: love deep, live hard, and have fun.

I find myself encouraging my clients to adopt some of these same attitudes. Plan, have a back-up plan, and then go live. Go do the things you can afford to do. Life will happen, regardless of how much you worry. So live it to its very fullest while you can.

## A CAREER TAKES SHAPE

I met my wife at Miami University when, as an accounting major, I applied to work in a student-run credit union. The person who interviewed me was Holli, whom I would marry soon after college. It was a great experience running a real financial institution with $2 million in student deposits. It was highly entrepreneurial. We dealt with the responsibility of serving customers, meeting regulatory standards, training employees, and all activities needed to run a real business. And we did all of this as volunteers! Our sole compensation was the incredible training and experience we were getting.

My intention was to become an accountant, and by the time I graduated in 1993, I had multiple offers to join prestigious firms as a CPA. I went to work for Deloitte & Touche where I learned many of the technical skills needed to be effective for my clients today. In my field, it's important to have a numbers background—but the numbers alone were not enough for me. I felt they must be used to serve and to change people's lives.

Holli had a different perspective. "I know you're smart," she said, "but you're going to be terrible at this CPA stuff. This is not who you are."

"Oh, I'll be fine," I told her. "I'll be partner someday, and we'll talk about it then."

She was right, as usual (my wife is right more often than I give her credit for). Accounting may be the language of business, but finance is where all those numbers are put to practical use. With that in mind, I left Deloitte to pursue my MBA at Indiana University.

Procter & Gamble called me one day with a job offer—not for a position in finance but in marketing and advertising. It wasn't the route I had been planning, but Holli worked at P&G, and this job would allow me to be back in Cincinnati with her. I began work there in 1997, but my mother died shortly afterward. Emotionally, I was a wreck, and it showed in my work. I ended up leaving P&G in 1998 to pursue work that was more core to who I am.

In grad school, I had done an internship with a Cincinnati company called Western & Southern Financial Group, a big company involved in many aspects of finance, including insurance, investments, and commercial real estate. I had been interested in the company's management training program until I was swayed by the Procter & Gamble offer, and now they were kind enough to let me back in.

I spent six years with Western & Southern, and that is where I got a lot of the grounding in what I do professionally for clients today. I learned a lot at that company—including what I did not want out of my life and career. I wanted something entrepreneurial. Not since my days at the student credit union had I felt that I was impacting the direction of a business. I wanted to truly get to know the customer and offer direct help. I knew that for me, a satisfying career would have both those elements.

I remember how nervous I felt when I went to tell my boss and my mentor, both wonderful guys, that I was leaving Western & Southern. I had been through so much with them, and they had put a lot of faith in me. I was making good money as an assistant vice president, and my job was secure, but I didn't feel fulfilled.

"I have this calling," I told them. "I need to be out there impacting other lives with my work." My boss completely understood; he seemed almost wistful, as if he had felt that calling himself. My mentor, I think, had long known me better than I knew myself. "I expected this someday," he said, "and you're right, Erik. You need to be an entrepreneur."

## THE ENTREPRENEURIAL CALL

I have learned that couples tend to complement each other. I saw it in my parents' marriage, and I certainly have seen it in my own. When Holli told me I wouldn't be happy as a CPA—and later at Procter & Gamble—she could see what I couldn't, that I would never be happy in a big, corporate environment. I needed to be on the front lines, seeing firsthand the impact of my work. I needed to combine my strong financial background with the life experiences that had shaped me and translate that into meaningful work on behalf of others. I had to start my own financial planning practice.

Life already was a swirl. Holli and I had one child with another on the way, and she was traveling widely for Procter & Gamble, working with international brands. But we had planned this move for a long time and had saved up. We knew that building a business demands effort and sacrifice, but when you're chasing your dreams, nothing can stop you.

I did well in my first year. In fact, I was named planner of the year for my region. It was right after that, in January 2005, when my father died. I felt devastated, even though we knew that the phone call would be coming one day. Throughout his illness, I served as my father's power of attorney, managing his care and his finances as best I could while trying to raise my own family. Upon his death, I served as executor of the estate. These experiences gave me firsthand insight into the difficulties clients face with aging and end-of-life issues. They allow me to truly understand and empathize with clients and make me a better advisor.

In time, I got my practice back on track and learned a lot about what it takes to be successful in this profession. Eventually I joined with a partner and laid the groundwork for what we today call Oxford Financial Partners. Today I bring to my clients all the professional and personal experiences that have shaped me. I have been battle tested and have come out stronger on the other side. Those successes and setbacks have enabled me to help clients of a variety of ages, including retirees, find their way. I get it. I understand the range of issues that people face. In the pages ahead I will show you how to effectively deal with them—not just to troubleshoot but to build confidently toward a prosperous future.

If you are ready to chart your own course toward retirement success, read on to learn how *Power of 5 Investing*® and Oxford Financial Partners can help you.

# INTRODUCTION

## *POWER OF 5 INVESTING®*

The simple pleasures in life, like quietly reading a book, often bring the most joy. I enjoy reading about history and the economy, so I recently searched online for some of the most popular titles on investment advice.

What I found was disturbing. Nearly every popular title on finance and the markets was built on doom and gloom. I suppose that's nothing new, but the Internet has made it that much easier to be connected to these doomsday forecasts via online books, newsletters, blogs, and videos.

As I continued looking at these titles, I realized that a formula was at work. I am now going to reveal to you how to write the next big business bestseller. It's actually not that difficult. You just need a catchy title; the content doesn't much matter.

Step 1:   You must refer to a recent problem by using one of the following words: "crash," "crisis," "aftershock," "collapse," "bubble," or "meltdown."

Step 2:   You must predict another crisis. Use words like "coming," "next," or "future." For extra flair, write that the problem will be "global."

Step 3:   Your book title must imply that you have a "survival guide" or "strategy" that will result in a "profit."

Most of those books do the same thing. They paint a horrible picture of the future, backed up by evidence of the recent horrible past, and then they reveal some magic formula for profiting from the next crisis. Such books are usually written by someone who wants to sell you a newsletter or manage your money.

What you often get are fancy words with a false premise. Most often, the core of the investment philosophy is a belief in timing the markets. The authors will claim to keep you out of stocks when things look risky and get you back into stocks (or whatever asset class is the flavor of the day) when the time is right. They probably believe they are correct—but they are delusional if they think they have the holy grail of investing. Nobody has found that, and nobody ever will.

This is the truth you need to know: The philosophy of buy and hold is not dead. What has worked is what will work. You need a proper allocation of stocks, bonds, and cash. You always need to own the stocks of well-run companies; that's where the growth has been. You should set aside five years' worth of income in stable investments and then invest the remainder in growth-focused investments. When you have gains in the latter, use them to replenish the former. Lather, rinse, repeat.

I suppose the authors of those doomsday books are smart in their own way. They scare people into action and thereby put lots of fees in their pockets. They prey on people's fears and set themselves up as the wizards who should be handling their money. They may be doing well for themselves, but they are lousy stewards of their clients' wealth. They are a cancer on my profession.

We don't have many clients who buy into this doom and gloom perspective. They know better, and that's why they sought us out. The doomsayers tend to attract their own kind. If you truly believe that the world's best investment is bottled water and the best strategy is to head for the hills, then you will look for compatriots who will support your stance. Unfortunately, as you jump from one hot idea to the next, you more than likely will do something with your money when you shouldn't or do nothing when you should.

I am an optimist at heart. I believe in the human spirit's ability to do far more than survive. We are meant to thrive. I believe that those who build upon that premise will be well on their way to the success of their dreams.

## FACING THE BIG DECISION

Most of our clients come to us in their 50s or 60s, thinking it's time to retire soon—either by their own choice or because their company is downsizing. They face a big decision coming up within a few years and are wondering how retirement will look for them. They want to know whether they will be all right. They typically have set aside a sum of money in a retirement fund. A few still have company pensions. We help them through the transitions and the worries and get them off to a good start with a solid portfolio.

We also serve people who have been retired for some time and feel reassured that their retirement plan is working. At that point, they sometimes are assessing whether they have made the right life choices. They often are trying to work out what their legacy will be.

Other clients include younger executives in their late 30s into their 40s who still are raising families and building. They have a lot of years of work ahead of them. They have questions about diversification and taxes and stock options. They are saving and investing *for* retirement, and we help set them on the proper course.

Investing *for* retirement is hard enough; investing *during* retirement is much more complex, and that's what this book is all about. As people reach retirement, the question isn't how they got to where they are. That's past. Now it's time to make their life savings last for what could be decades longer through the ups and downs of the market and through all that life will throw at them.

That's where we can make a difference. *Power of 5 Investing* was built specifically with retirees in mind.

## FIVE POWERFUL PRINCIPLES

In this book, I will share with you the principles we developed that have served our clients well for years. Our shorthand way to refer to those principles is *Power of 5 Investing*—and that is not some mystical mantra. These are five powerful principles for a successful retirement.

I saw the power of these principles during what has been popularly dubbed the Great Recession in 2008 and 2009. "I've never seen so many people so terrified of what the future will hold," observed one of my staff members, a woman with thirty years in the business.

We take pride in being a rock for people through good times and bad, and we certainly felt the weight of that role then. There were days when I spent hours on the phone, showing people exactly how *Power of 5 Investing* was helping to protect their retirement even during a severe market correction. We got people through those times—and erased any doubts they might have had about their financial future. It was our trial by fire. We followed our process without deviating from it. And, yes, that was a very painful recession, but our clients still stand strong. They are not scrambling for some magic formula that will save their skin. They are not chasing some fad. They have found confidence in solid good sense: if it worked through those times, they figure, it will work through anything.

## FIVE POWERFUL PRINCIPLES

In the chapters ahead, we'll take a close look at each principle of *Power of 5 Investing*:

## FIVE STEPS OF INVESTING

In chapter 1, we'll look at a disciplined, five-step process in managing your investments. We'll explore the importance of (a) advice and planning, (b) portfolio modeling and design, (c) manager search and selection, (d) implementation, and (e) monitoring and reporting.

## LIVING ON **FIVE PERCENT**

Getting the annual withdrawal rate right is far and away the biggest determinant of your retirement success. In chapter 2, we'll look at why a withdrawal rate between 4 and 6 percent could be appropriate for most retirees.

## **FIVE YEARS** OF STABILITY

You will learn in chapter 3 about how our "Stability Bucket" takes the emotion out of retirement investing. In short, set aside five years of your withdrawal needs in low-volatility investments, and devote the rest of your portfolio to growth. In a bear market, the money in your Stability Bucket will help you ignore the temptation to sell growth investments at fire-sale prices.

## THE **FIVE PERCENT** LIMIT

We believe that no single growth holding should represent more than 5 percent of your portfolio. Diversifying your portfolio is critically important, and you need to maintain that balance periodically.

## FIVE WORDS OF WISDOM

"It's *never* different this time." In a bear market, people who think that this time is different, and that the market won't bounce back, sell their stocks to people who understand that this time is never different. *Power of 5 Investing* stands steadfastly with the optimists.

## A STEADYING INFLUENCE

This book is your alternative to all those doom and gloom volumes out there. What I offer here is solid knowledge and experience, not the sensational solutions that capture so much attention.

There's a lot of noise out there. The Internet has transformed the world, opening the power of information in amazing ways. However, it also has become a venue for the dissemination of much nonsense. Every talking head or columnist seems to profess a different strategy. "Roboadvisors" claim to offer personalized investment advice via nothing more than some mysterious computer in the cloud. None of them know you personally and truly understand your unique needs, and yet they seem to set themselves up as financial wizards. No matter how outrageous, some people will believe that it must be true.

A healthy sense of skepticism has always been wise, and in today's informational avalanche, it is essential. Perhaps there was a time, at the apex of journalistic integrity, when people could trust much of what they read in print. But today, it is easier than ever to dispense garbage. You need to follow a set of clear principles so the media noise won't get in the way of your progress.

People sometimes ask us whether we have some trick to gauging the market. We have no wand or crystal ball. Think of us as your partners. We do our utmost to help you find the right strategy—and rather than a trick, that requires a good measure of sense. We do not know, nor does anyone, exactly what the future holds at any particular time. *Power of 5 Investing* builds portfolios in anticipation of market volatility, not in reaction to it.

That's an approach that explicitly recognizes and deals with the truth that the market can be capricious. The bad times come regularly. We don't know exactly when the economy will turn, but when it does, our clients will be positioned to persevere and prosper.

Many people find it tough to resist the temptation to make a rash move in a bear market as the media noise becomes deafening. If you are uncertain you have that discipline, we offer the kind of professional guidance that can help you. People hire specialists all the time to handle tasks that require specialized knowledge or that (for whatever reason) they don't want to do themselves. Wise leaders delegate. If that is your choice, we can give you knowledgeable and experienced advice on how to attain a fruitful retirement through *Power of 5 Investing*.

Our most valuable service is not what you might think. It's not how we model whether you are on track for retirement. It's not how we build your portfolio optimally, with the right managers. Our most valuable service is that we are a steadying force through good times and bad. We keep people on track with the plan that they agreed was the one that made sense to them. We provide continuing guidance and coaching and help you develop the discipline to fend off the temptations.

The bottom line is always going to be trust. It should be a given that your advisor will take good care of your money. What will keep you coming back is the reassurance that the advisor cares about you. The analytical approach only goes so far. We seek long-term relationships with our clients. You want someone who has got your back—not just your account.

# CHAPTER 1

## *FIVE STEPS* OF INVESTING

I recently met with a divorced mother of two teenage daughters. The girls were both very bright, and their mother was looking forward to sending them to excellent universities, but the cost of college was very worrisome to her. Where would she get the money? She figured something had to give, and so she had been sacrificing her contributions to her retirement savings. She planned to continue funneling her excess money into college savings with the hope that if she hired us we could really jump-start the returns on her retirement contributions after the girls graduated.

That's a common reaction among parents in their 40s and 50s. They want the best for their children; they don't want them to enter the world with any financial burdens. We understand that. They also feel they can deal with retirement later; after all, college is coming up quickly, but retirement may be 10–20 years away. But we know it doesn't work that way. You can always borrow money for college expenses, but who will lend you half a million for retirement that you can pay back later?

I asked her about retirement. When did she hope to retire, how much had she saved so far, how much was she contributing to her 401(k), how was it invested, etc. She said she wanted to retire at 62 but had no idea how that was going to happen. She also indicated she was not comfortable with the markets, despite what had been an incredible five-year run of nearly straight up growth in the US stock market.

She had so many unanswered questions. Her fear of the unknown had paralyzed her into taking practically no action whatsoever on her retirement. She needed a plan. Over time, we introduced her to the same powerful ideas we will share with you in this book; she got comfortable with our approach and was able to move past her initial paralysis.

Our very first job, long before we talk specifically about investments, is to get people on track to achieving their goals. That starts with asking lots of questions, getting to know the person. From there we can develop a plan to get them to where they want to go.

So many people are afraid to make a plan because they suspect they aren't on track. It can be embarrassing and uncomfortable; that's understandable. Nobody wants to be told they have done a bad job. No one wants to hear bad news. But until you know where you stand, how can you do anything about it? To me, no news at all is far worse than bad news. Bad news is not failure. Bad news we can fix. No news leads to inaction, and inaction is almost certainly a ticket to failure.

You know where you stand through the big-picture advice and planning we offer you. We seek to understand who you are and where you want to be. We find out how much risk you and your portfolio can tolerate. We figure your income requirements during retirement; and we look at how much access you will need to liquid money assets. We write all of this down in an easy-to-follow format. This plan then becomes the basis from which we can design your investment portfolio.

## THE FIVE-STEP PROCESS

If you have a disciplined process and you follow it, you get good results. *Power of 5 Investing* leverages solid financial planning and takes it to the next level. In this chapter, we'll take a close look at the first of those five principles: the five steps of investing.

THE 5-STEP PROCESS

STEP 1
Advice and Planning

STEP 2
Portfolio modeling and design

STEP 3
Manager search and selection

STEP 4
Implementation

STEP 5
Monitoring and reporting

# STEP ONE:
# ADVICE AND PLANNING

The very first step is building a plan. If you don't have a plan, you are not going to know what you are shooting for or whether you are on track.

Our established clients, for the most part, have long since resolved how much money they will have for retirement and from where it will come. We already have a plan in place, and the task at hand becomes one of monitoring and adjusting. Newer clients, however, need to start with building a comprehensive plan.

Our financial planning process begins with a proprietary tool we call the Personal Financial Portal℠. Here we gather all of your financial information in one place, showing us the resources available to support your retirement needs. It updates as the markets change and as you add contributions. It helps us monitor your progress toward retirement each year.

The Personal Financial Portal is also where we build the financial plan and deliver it to you. Let's say you are 54 and plan to save an additional $1,000 a month and hope to reach a retirement target at 65. We can model how to direct that money to meet your retirement goal, and we can see how all your other assets play into meeting your goal as well.

## A Note: The Five Parts of Step One

In our financial planning work, we look at five major areas:

*Estate Planning*—Are my will, trust, living will, and powers of attorney still in good order? Are my beneficiary designations consistent with my estate documents?

*Risk Management*—Do I have sufficient life insurance so that my family is protected? Are long-term care and disability income insurance appropriate for my situation?

*Retirement Planning*—Am I saving enough *for* retirement? Am I withdrawing too much *in* retirement? When should I exercise my stock options, and what should I do with the proceeds?

*Cash Flow Management and Taxes*—Will I have enough income in retirement? How will Social Security affect my retirement? How should I plan for taxes?

*Investment Management Strategies*—Is my portfolio properly allocated? How are my investments doing? Are changes needed?

All five of these areas are incredibly important and interrelated. Of the five general areas for review, notice how we make investments the very last one. That's not because investments aren't important;

it's because they always seem to be where many clients want to start, but we make sure they first consider all the other planning elements. The plan drives the investment decisions, not the other way around. As a CERTIFIED FANANCIAL PLANNER™ professional, I do a lot more than just handle investments. Getting people on the right track comes first.

So while this book focuses on the five powerful principles for retirement investing, remember that investing is only *one* part of financial planning. If you're working with someone who only wants to talk about your investments, it's time to look for a different advisor.

## THE IMMOVABLE OBJECT MEETS
## THE UNSTOPPABLE FORCE

*Power of 5 Investing* rests on a foundation of a thoughtful plan—but you can't build a plan unless you are realistic about the possibilities and clearly understand how you are doing. I'm comfortable with giving people the unvarnished truth—and I know we have driven some people away when we gave them the facts.

One couple contacted us for some advice about whether the wife should accept a voluntary early retirement package as severance from her company. They were in their late 50s, with children still finishing college.

"I've decided I'm taking it," the wife told me, "but I just wanted to check with somebody before I did it." She already had her wish list ready to go. "I'm getting a year of severance and something from my stock options," she said—and in her mind she had it all spent as she thought about the fun things she would do.

"We've worked hard all these years, and we deserve some things." That word "deserve" came up quite a bit. "There's this beach house in North Carolina that we've been renting, and we figure buy it now that I've got this severance package. Because we've earned it."

It's not uncommon. We all dream of things we might do, but we also need to take a longer-term perspective. It's great to be 58 and spending money and feeling good—but how will you be feeling when you are 85 and most of your money is gone?

We met with that couple and took very careful notes. We sent them a letter in which we detailed what we heard them say about their wants and needs, as well as what we had learned from their tax return about their actual income and spending.

"I don't see how this is going to work," I wrote in the letter. "You told us you plan to buy that beach house for $300,000, but that's money you could instead be using to support your income needs in retirement."

People get a sense of entitlement. They feel that they have worked hard and deserve their big reward. Often it's quite true that they worked hard, but they should only lay claim to what the money has the power to accomplish. If the most important goal is maintaining an accustomed lifestyle in retirement and not running out of money, then that should be reward enough.

Our advice in the letter was that she should not take that severance package and that they should not buy the beach house. The numbers just didn't add up to a successful retirement. That couple didn't hire us. We gave them the bad news, and they chose to ignore it. They did not hire us, and that's just as well—we cannot work with those who are unwilling to face the truth. I tell people what they *need* to hear, not what they *want* to hear. If they don't want to hear it, there's not much I can do to help them.

## STEP TWO:
## PORTFOLIO MODELING AND DESIGN

Once we come to an understanding about your goals, then the next step is to decide what the investment plan to support them would look like.

During the advice and planning phase in the first step, we spend a considerable amount of time getting to know you, understanding your retirement goals, time horizon, and eventual cash flow needs. We will also have an in-depth discussion of the risks inherent with retirement investing, demonstrating what can happen to the portfolio when the inevitable market corrections come. Only then will we design (or revise) the investment plan. We document this in a written Investment Policy Statement (IPS). The IPS documents the outcomes that the portfolio must generate to support the retirement goals documented in the financial planning phase.

## Allocation Comparison | Prepared for Joe and Jane Smith

*This report compares your current portfolio's allocation with that of your target portfolio.*

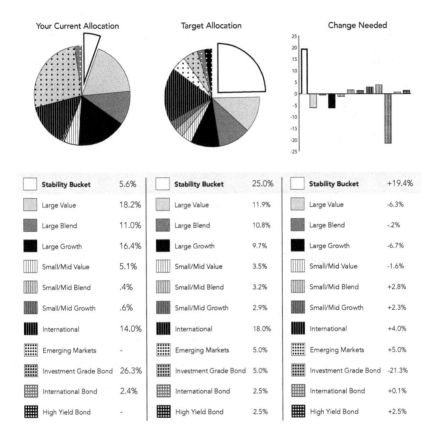

| | Your Current Allocation | | Target Allocation | | Change Needed |
|---|---|---|---|---|---|
| Stability Bucket | 5.6% | Stability Bucket | 25.0% | Stability Bucket | +19.4% |
| Large Value | 18.2% | Large Value | 11.9% | Large Value | -6.3% |
| Large Blend | 11.0% | Large Blend | 10.8% | Large Blend | -.2% |
| Large Growth | 16.4% | Large Growth | 9.7% | Large Growth | -6.7% |
| Small/Mid Value | 5.1% | Small/Mid Value | 3.5% | Small/Mid Value | -1.6% |
| Small/Mid Blend | .4% | Small/Mid Blend | 3.2% | Small/Mid Blend | +2.8% |
| Small/Mid Growth | .6% | Small/Mid Growth | 2.9% | Small/Mid Growth | +2.3% |
| International | 14.0% | International | 18.0% | International | +4.0% |
| Emerging Markets | - | Emerging Markets | 5.0% | Emerging Markets | +5.0% |
| Investment Grade Bond | 26.3% | Investment Grade Bond | 5.0% | Investment Grade Bond | -21.3% |
| International Bond | 2.4% | International Bond | 2.5% | International Bond | +0.1% |
| High Yield Bond | - | High Yield Bond | 2.5% | High Yield Bond | +2.5% |

The IPS includes a side-by-side comparison that says, in effect, "This is you right now, this is how you should look, and here are the recommended changes." It looks at your portfolio at a macro level (i.e., your asset allocation among stocks/bonds/cash) and at a micro level (how many dollars are in a particular investment). On the left is your current portfolio. On the right is our recommended portfolio. If there is a difference between the two columns, we will provide specific buys or sells to bring the portfolio back into balance with your plan.

So, let's say you have a reasonable set of goals, the time is right, and our analysis indicates that your plan will work. This step makes sure that your portfolio is designed to properly meet your objectives and grow adequately. And for those already retired, this step looks at whether the plan is reliably providing the designated amount of dollars required for you to live on. For clients who have been with us for a while, we already know their goals and have documented them. We now are looking for whatever tweaks the portfolio needs to continue supporting those goals.

## STEP THREE:
## MANAGER SEARCH AND SELECTION

Now that we know what the rough outline looks like, we need to fill in the details. At this point, you might be saying, "Okay, I agree with you that this is how my portfolio should look, and yes we need 30 percent in US large stocks. Tell me what to put it in." That's where the third step comes in.

There are many types of investments and approaches that can be used effectively in *Power of 5 Investing*, depending on your situation. What is essential is that the portfolio be built with a healthy dose of stocks at all times, good and bad. The power of stocks to deliver a successful retirement is covered more fully in chapters 3 and 5.

There are a lot of investment research tools out there, and some may be better than others for your purposes. We sift through the many options so that we can recommend the investments that we believe would be appropriate for you. We recommend the proper proportion of those investments and the managers who we feel are suited for the task. We get into the nitty-gritty of choosing the right way to implement the portfolio. Now it's time for action.

......................................................................................

## A Word on Asset Allocation and Security Selection

The second step in the investment process is about asset allocation—maintaining the proper balance among broad asset classes like stocks, bonds, and cash. The third step is all about security selection—choosing the investment vehicles to support the asset allocation targets from the second step.

At this point, you're probably wondering:

1) How do you know which asset classes to use in the "Growth Bucket?"

2) How much money should go into each asset class?

3) How do you go about choosing which investments to use to fill out the asset allocation?

These are all excellent questions, and the answers truly matter, but they are outside the scope of this book. What matters here is gaining a full understanding of the principles outlined in *Power of 5 Investing* and ensuring they are implemented in a way that helps you achieve your goals. A number of excellent books on asset allocation and security selection can be found in chapter 8.

......................................................................................

## STEP FOUR:
## IMPLEMENTATION

The implementation of those decisions made in the third step is actually a pretty short phase. By this time, we have completed the first step and done the upfront planning to determine and document goals. We know what we need to accomplish and what it will take to get there. In the second step, we built the outline of how the portfolio would look and developed an investment plan to meet those goals. And in the third step, we screened the universe of available investments to provide written recommendations about how much to put into specific investments to support the plan. Now it's time to tie it all together. In the implementation step, we put the plan into action. For a step-by-step example, see chapter 6.

## STEP FIVE:
## MONITORING AND REPORTING

Contrary to popular wisdom, there are three—not two—universal truths. Yes, there are death and taxes. But there's also change. Your plan and your advisor must account for that. That's where the fifth step comes in. Your plan has to be watched. Someone needs to monitor it and check it against your original intentions.

There are several aspects to monitoring and reporting:

1. Are you meeting the savings targets that you documented?

2. How is your Stability Bucket doing?

3. Is your overall asset allocation still in balance?

4. How have the investment vehicles that you chose been doing against their benchmarks?

5. Do you have a reporting system in place that can track all of this for you and alert you to changes that may be needed?

6. Are you reviewing these reports on a consistent basis?

7. When action is warranted, do you have the discipline to take corrective action?

Once the plan is built and documented in the Personal Financial Portal, we then monitor your progress via a proprietary tool we call The Financial Wellcheck$^{SM}$. This tool summarizes your entire financial life on one piece of paper, with clear visual cues of stop/caution/go to show if you are on track and whether an action needs to be taken.

When you are due for an annual review, we'll reach out about six weeks in advance and send a checklist across those major areas. We ask if anything has changed in your life—new needs, new grandchildren, an upcoming wedding, etc. After you send that information, we go to work right away and consider the range of issues. We'll develop an agenda well in advance of the meeting and tailor it to your needs. We'll update The Financial Wellcheck to reflect any new choices or developments and use this as the basis for our meeting together.

# THE FINANCIAL WELLCHECK℠

Client: Joe & Jane Smith
Date: July 2014

| FINANCIAL AREA | CRITICAL COMPONENTS | | NEXT STEPS |
|---|---|---|---|
| **Estate Planning** | | | |
| a) Estate Documents | Will, Living Will, Power of Attorney, Health Care Proxy, Trusts (2008 - Attorney name here) | | |
| b) Beneficiary Designation | IRA 1: Primary: Joe 100%; Contingent: Fred 50%, Mary 50% | | |
| | IRA 2: Primary: Joe 100%; Contingent: Not listed | **STOP** | Need Contingent |
| **Risk Management** | | | |
| a) Life Insurance | Lincoln Life, $1,500,000 death benefit, owned by trust | | Continue Funding |
| b) Long Term Care | N/A - Discussed at 2009 meeting; determined that coverage too expensive | | |
| c) Disability Income | N/A (retired) | | |
| **Retirement/Education Planning** | | | |
| a) Retirement Progress | Current / 3-year withdrawal rates: 5.1% / 4.9% | | |
| b) Employee Stock Options | See attached analysis | **CAUTION** | |
| c) Education Planning | Education goals achieved<br>Assumed $25,000/yr. tuition, 5% inflation, $250/mo. contribution, 6.7% growth | | Continue Funding |
| **Cash Flow Management** | | | |
| a) Distributions and Taxes | **Current Monthly Cash flow** | | |
| | Jane IRA Distribution | $5,000 | |
| | Less 20% federal / 5% state taxes | ($1,250) | |
| | **Net deposit to client** | **$3,750** | |
| b) Required Minimum Distribution | **$55,357 for 2014; satisfied by monthly distributions ($60,000)** | | |
| c) Tax Reduction Strategies | Capital gains tax avoided of $8,698 from PG sales made in 2013 | | |
| **Investment Management Strategies** | | | |
| a) Goals Documented | Investment Policy Statement dated 3/15/13 | | |
| b) Portfolio Returns | Lifetime Return (1996): Deposits $2,000,000; Withdrawals $1,000,000; Current $2,550,000 | | |
| | Three year average annual return (after fees and expenses): 8.2% | | |
| c) Power of 5 Investing® | 5% withdrawal rate | | |
| | 5 years stability bucket | | |
| | **5% diversification limit: Client desires 10% PG position** | **CAUTION** | |
| d) Portfolio Rebalancing | See attached proposal | **CAUTION** | Joe & Jane sign proposal |

## WHEN PRIORITIES CHANGE

Even if you are attending to all of those challenges, are you modifying your plans in light of significant life events? You get a big inheritance. You lose a job. Your spouse dies. When such things happen, you need to consider how they will affect your overall planning strategy.

In other words, those five steps do not end at the last one. You need to go back to the first step. The five steps are a cycle. When we meet annually, we will circle back to that first step and discuss whether anything has changed. It could have been something joyous or something tragic, but in any case, the repercussions can be significant, and we need to know about it. If there have been no significant changes, then we can be confident that the plan is sound and may need only some tweaking.

Plans change only when goals change. Plans do not change because the stock market is too high/low or a new virus spreads or a government is overthrown or a commodity becomes scarce or for any other short-term reason, no matter how scary it may seem. Your goal is to retire reasonably young, live comfortably, and die with your dignity intact, hopefully with few financial worries along the way. Your goal has a 30–50-year time horizon, and your plan should be just as long-lived and rock solid. *Power of 5 Investing* ensures that the foundational plan is in place.

The first pillar, the five-step investing process, is crucial to laying the foundation for a successful retirement. In chapter 2, we will explore what kind of cash flow one can expect from his or her portfolio in retirement.

# CHAPTER 2

## LIVING ON *FIVE PERCENT*

A large number of couples who have come through our doors fit this portrait: they saved for decades, aware that they needed to put together a nest egg big enough so that they could make withdrawals for retirement income each year while not depleting the balance too much.

Every financial planner has encountered countless couples like that, filled with hope for a fruitful retirement and yet grappling with uncertainty. They might come in with a portfolio of a million dollars. "We're millionaires!" they say. "Surely, we're set for life—right?" Until we take a closer look, there's not much I can say except, "Well, that depends."

It depends, indeed, on a number of factors: How long will the couple live? One or the other or both will likely need an income for decades to come in retirement. And how much of an income are they expecting? Often they do not really know, except they typically figure they'll probably need less than they did during their working years. But will they? Many people want to travel or purchase a second home or spend a lot more time on hobbies (which can be expensive) or leave large sums of money for their grandchildren. Is that going to be less to live on than when they were working?

It also depends on what other income sources they might have. How much do they expect in Social Security benefits? Is there a pension? Do they have any 401(k)s or other such retirement plans? Does either spouse intend to keep working to some extent? And how much does the couple hope to leave to heirs or to charity? Do they expect to preserve their nest egg principal for the kids?

In our experience, the right answer for most retirees is one that leverages their guaranteed income sources, such as pensions and Social Security, and supplements them with a reasonable withdrawal from their retirement nest egg. *Power of 5 Investing* maintains that retirees, depending on their situation, can withdraw around 5 percent (ranging from 4 percent to 6 percent) of their retirement assets each year with a very high potential of enjoying a successful retirement. In this chapter, we will take a look at how we determine that rate and how to put it into action as a key determinant of retirement success.

## CASH FLOW IN RETIREMENT

Retirees may have several sources of cash flow in retirement. Most often these include:

1. ***Social Security.*** Despite much bad press about the shaky finances of the Social Security system, the reality for today's retirees is that Social Security can represent a meaningful source of guaranteed, inflation-adjusted income. According to a study published in *USA Today* in October 2014[1], the average retired couple today takes home $2,140 per month in Social Security payments. That's easily $25,000 per year that the portfolio doesn't have to generate.

2. ***Pension.*** While the notion of putting in 30 years for one company and getting a gold watch and pension seems quaint these days, pensions can still represent a significant source of cash flow for certain retirees. Teachers, firefighters, police, military, and other public service employees can sometimes maintain as much as 80 percent of their preretirement income. Private sector pensions, however, are quickly vanishing and may be a prelude to the end of pensions for most of today's younger workers.

3. ***Part-time work.*** More and more we are seeing retirees in their mid-50s being offered an early retirement incentive package, only to be offered their job back a year later as a consultant. Many times the hourly pay is the same and the hours are more flexible, they just don't have fringe benefits. Younger retirees in particular should look for opportunities to redeploy their experience and skills at another employer; they are often surprised at how many contacts they have and how much they can make.

---

1 "Social Security benefits get another tiny raise" John Waggoner, USA TODAY 4:50 p.m. EDT October 23, 2014

4. *Deferred compensation and stock options.* While not as common, some retirees have the ability to generate cash flow from their prior work years. This can allow the retirement portfolio to stay intact longer and generate more growth before beginning distributions.

5. *Retirement portfolio withdrawals.* Today's reality is that retirement portfolio withdrawals are usually the most significant source of cash flow in retirement. *Power of 5 Investing* was built to deal specifically with this complex issue.

## A REASONABLE WITHDRAWAL RATE

Because withdrawals from the retirement portfolio play such a huge role in the cash flow plans of today's and tomorrow's retirees, it's important to get this right. The right withdrawal rate generates enough income for the retiree to live comfortably today, while also generating the growth needed to meet cash flow needs as much as 30 or 40 years into the future. This is no small task.

Why is this so difficult? Because people are retiring earlier and living longer than they used to. According to the Society of Actuaries study *2011 Risks and Process of Retirement Survey,* life spans are continuing to increase. In the past half-century, life expectancy for newborn American males improved by an average of almost two years each decade, from 66.6 years in 1960 to 75.7 years by 2010. For females, the average increase was about 1.5 years per decade, from 73.1 years in 1960 to 80.8 years by 2010.  Furthermore, by age

65, US males in average health have a 40 percent chance of living to age 85 and females more than a 50 percent chance. The survivor of a 65-year-old couple is more than 70 percent likely to reach 85. For healthier people, even a 25 percent reduction in mortality increases those chances to 50 percent for males, 62 percent for females, and 81 percent for the survivor. That means the average person can expect to live to age 85 or beyond! Which side of average are you on?

Determining the withdrawal rate becomes an art as well as a science. It's based on an assessment of longevity that nobody knows for certain. That's why our 5 percent withdrawal rate is actually the average of what we recommend, and we are conservative. Most people would far rather leave this world with a little bit of cash left over than spend the last years of their lives wondering how to pay the bills—or being financially dependent on someone else.

The following chart is an overview of how we look at "safe" withdrawal rates. Of course, nobody knows exactly how much longer they will live, but we have found these guidelines to be prudent in our experience with clients and in light of Americans' ever increasing longevity:

| Client Age | Expected Longevity | Withdrawal Rate |
|------------|-------------------|-----------------|
| 50 | 35-40 years | 3.5% |
| 55 | 30-35 years | 4.0% |
| 65 | 20-25 years | 5.0% |
| 75 | 10-15 years | 6.0% |

# HISTORY OF THE "SAFE" WITHDRAWAL RATE

Research into the safe withdrawal rate for retirees has been an area of intensive research for both academics and practitioners for more than two decades now. Yet there is plenty of interpretation as to just what the correct rate may be. Note that the term "safe" here refers to a rate that is designed to provide income for a typical life expectancy. When it comes to investing, there is nothing that is truly safe.

The original research in this area is generally attributed to researcher William P. Bengen, a now retired financial planner, who published his findings in 1994 in the *Journal of Financial Planning*. Bengen popularized the 4 percent safe withdrawal rate that is often mentioned in the press. This 4 percent rule suggests you can initially withdraw 4 percent of your retirement account without worrying that you will outlive your money. In addition, and this is a very key point, the research assumes that your initial 4 percent withdrawal amount can be increased for inflation each year. If we assume the client starts with a $1 million retirement portfolio, then their first year with-drawal would be $40,000 ($1,000,000 * 4 percent). If inflation was 3 percent, then the client's second year withdrawal would be $41,200 ($40,000 * 1.03).

Bengen conducted extensive research to show what would have happened to his clients' portfolios had they followed his 4 percent rule even in the face of an awful bear market. To test his concept, he looked at what happened to those who retired in 1971, right before the '73–74 bear market.

The '70s were bad enough with the bellbottoms, wide collars, leisure suits, and disco (I still cringe when I see those pictures of myself as a kid—who dressed me like *that*?). Adding insult to injury, we experienced the oil shocks of '73 and '79, long lines at the gas pumps, and some of the worst blizzards in recorded history. The US economy struggled to grow, and even our own President Carter lamented our "crisis of confidence" and "growing doubt about the meaning of our own lives."

For investors, it was likewise bleak. Retirees back then might well have had a pension to sustain them, but it was an awful time to be invested in the stock market. If you bought a basket of stocks in the early '70s and looked at your portfolio in 1980 after those Jimmy Carter years, the price of those shares had hardly budged at all. Sure, you pocketed some dividends, but there really was no growth in the prices. It was a miserable time, but Bengen discovered that retirees following his 4 percent rule would have made it through that terrible time and had their portfolio last a full 30 years of retirement. In the years since Bengen published his original research, he has revisited his conclusions, and other academics have added their own perspectives. It's a hot topic, and the research continues. In his 2006 book *Conserving Client Portfolios During Retirement*, Bengen wrote, "The original 4 percent rule has moved much closer to a 5 percent rule."

Bengen updated his research once again in 2011 to reflect more recent market disruptions, including the dot-com meltdown, the 9/11 tragedy, and the Great Recession of 2008–2009. In his review, he concluded that, despite all of these market-shaking events, his prescribed withdrawal rate still had left retirees with sizable nest eggs. They had not run out of money before running out of time.

If anything, he said, he had been wrong. He felt that he had been too conservative in his recommendation and that they could have withdrawn more.

Many respected academics and practitioners such as Wade Pfau, Moshe Milevsky, Michael Kitces, Harold Evensky, Jonathan Guyton, Robert Veres, and David Blanchett continue to study the issue. Some suggest 4 percent is too high, while others have devised approaches with withdrawal rates exceeding 7 percent in certain circumstances. We are grateful to all the researchers for their ongoing contribution to our profession's body of knowledge. Their work has certainly informed some of the principles in *Power of 5 Investing*.

While we respect the hard work of the academics, we know there is a big difference between the hypothetical models so many academics cook up and the real world that we live in. The academics' models might be precise, but they fail to account for the emotional reactions that we experience when markets take a tumble—like in the '70s or during the 2008–2009 crisis. Many of the models also require clients to take a pay cut when the markets don't perform well. We find that people like predictable cash flow and straightforward explanations of how much money they can take out each year. All of the fancy models in the world don't mean a thing if they don't help you translate the research into meaningful action.

*Power of 5 Investing* leverages significant ongoing academic research and marries it with our years of real world experience. Our approach seeks to strike a practical balance between stability and growth over a few decades of retirement. A comfortable income for a lifetime, with maybe something left over for future generations—

that's what retirement success looks like to me, and that's what *Power of 5 Investing* is designed to deliver.

While there can be no assurance that some future retirement period won't be as bad or worse and understanding, of course, that past performance is not a guarantee of future results, we can all take some comfort in knowing that *Power of 5 Investing*'s 5 percent withdrawal principle has worked in some pretty rough times.

## YOUR WITHDRAWAL RATE IN ACTION

Once you have determined your withdrawal rate, how do you put it into action? The steps are relatively simple. By multiplying the rate times your retirement savings, you come up with the annual sum that you can reasonably withdraw from your portfolio each year for income. For example, if you have $1,200,000 in your retirement savings and have decided that a 5 percent withdrawal rate is right for you, then you can plan on withdrawing $60,000 per year ($1,200,000 * 5 percent). Is that sum, combined with your other sources of retirement income, enough for you to live on? If it is—and be sure to take taxes into account—then you can move onward into retirement. If it is not, then you need to keep working.

Your appropriate withdrawal rate is predicated upon having a healthy dose of stocks in your portfolio at all times. Why is that so important? Because inflation is the biggest threat to your retirement, and history has shown us that a diversified portfolio of the stocks of well-run companies has been the single best hedge you have against that threat. No other asset class on the planet has shown such an enduring ability to slay the inflation dragon.

In our experience, retiree portfolios are best served with as little as 50 percent to as much as 85 percent stocks *at all times* throughout retirement. These stocks comprise the bulk of what we call the Growth Bucket, balanced at all times with a lower volatility Stability Bucket. Withdrawals are taken regularly from the Stability Bucket, with the Stability Bucket strategically replenished by harvesting gains in the Growth Bucket. These concepts are described more fully in chapter 3.

## A RAISE FOR INFLATION?

A common question is whether you should get automatic raises to compensate for inflation. In other words, if the government says inflation in the past year was 3 percent and last year's withdrawal was $60,000, then your new withdrawal for the coming year would be $61,800 ($60,000 * 1.03). Inflation is up, so I should get a raise, right?

In years of working with retirees, we have found automatic raises for inflation to be unnecessary. Most retirees aren't facing an increase in housing costs because they either have paid off the mortgage or have a fixed rate. Medical-related inflation could be significant for some people later in their retirement, but many health-care expenses have been adequately covered by Medicare. Instead, their biggest inflationary expenses will be things such as food, gas, and travel, which tend to be a smaller part of their total spending. So, if retiree inflation isn't running all that high, why take money out of the retirement portfolio before you have to? We find it is better to leave the money in the portfolio to continue working and potentially growing for you.

We suggest you calculate your withdrawal rate on the day you retire and then take out that same number of dollars each year. When you do that, an interesting thing happens. You discover you can get along just fine on that fixed amount. We see it all the time with our clients. Meanwhile, the money not withdrawn creates a de facto emergency fund that you can call upon when one of life's little problems pops up. The furnace goes out, the roof needs a repair, the car won't start, or one of your kids needs your help. We handle these as a onetime distribution and keep the base withdrawal the same.

This hidden emergency fund, if not withdrawn, could really add up over time. As a hypothetical example, let's assume you retire with $1 million and plan to withdraw 5 percent of the portfolio in the first year. The portfolio grows at 6 percent per year, and inflation is 3 percent. You elect to take annual raises for inflation. After ten years, the portfolio has an ending value of $1,001,269 or about where it started. But what if you hadn't taken those automatic raises? The portfolio would be worth $1,092,266. That's an extra $90,000 available to you for emergencies. If you are like many of our clients, you will like knowing this extra is there for you.

## THE MAJOR FACTOR YOU CONTROL

There are many factors that go into a successful retirement:

- Setting goals
- Having a plan and sticking to it
- Building a properly diversified portfolio
- Choosing good investments

A good advisor can help you with all of the above, but the one factor that is uniquely in your hands is the withdrawal rate. Do yourself a favor—start with a reasonable withdrawal rate and stick with it.

We understand that life happens. Perhaps one of the children needs some special help. Perhaps you get hit with a serious illness that derails some of your plans. These things come up; you cannot predict them, but you can anticipate and prepare for them. By keeping your withdrawal rate at an agreed to and reasonable level from the beginning, we can help keep these things from having a catastrophic impact on your portfolio and retirement plans.

Again—let me repeat—your withdrawal rate is the major factor for your success that you control. We take care of the investments and discuss with you the potential tax consequences, and all the rest. That's our job. Abiding by a reasonable withdrawal rate is the best thing you can do to set yourself up for retirement success.

There is more than the withdrawal rate to consider, however. Those withdrawals need to be managed in a way that acknowledges market risk and anticipates it. In the next chapter, we'll discuss this further.

# CHAPTER 3

## *FIVE YEARS* OF STABILITY

E very portfolio we build for our clients is customized to their needs, risk tolerance level, and specifications. But while the details are customized, we believe in some core elements that are critical; one of these is that we believe it is essential to build five years of stability into every retirement plan. Even when the economy is humming along, you can be sure that the time will come when it will be dragging. You need protection so you can weather the bad times without panic or worry.

A new client and her husband had a sizable portfolio but not much in the way of income. As they neared retirement, that portfolio would need to sustain them in the years ahead. They had been working with a well-respected bank trust department, but nobody there had helped with their planning. Nobody had asked them when they intended to start drawing on the account and how much they would need every month.

I found that disturbing. In their situation, they needed the confidence of having several years' worth of their income needs set aside in an account that would not be at the mercy of the markets. We call that the Stability Bucket—and we always recommend that it contain five years of your upcoming cash flow needs. That's right—five full years of cash flow.

This couple had nothing of the sort; they had zero stability. We pointed out that shortcoming and the risk to which they were exposing themselves.

"Okay, I get it—I understand we need some stability in our portfolio," she said. "But do we really have to have five years' worth of it? That money's going to be sitting relatively idle. The market's growing leaps and bounds right now, and this Stability Bucket isn't going to be growing much. Aren't we missing out?"

"Well, of course you'd like to have the growth," I said, "and if we knew the market was going to be straight up from here, it'd be silly to have five years of stability. But if the past few years have taught us anything, it's that we don't know when the periods of market growth and constriction are going to occur—and that's why you need the Stability Bucket. That's the whole point."

I related to that woman what had happened to one of our particularly astute clients. He enjoys investing and dives deep into his prospectuses (those really long, and frequently very technical, booklets you receive from your investment companies outlining the construction of certain investments and listing their fees, charges and other expenses). He had never had five years of stability, as he did not want to miss out on market growth. Despite our reservations, he asked us to run his portfolio with only two years of stability. He was bright and well-informed and assured us he understood the risk. Then 2008 and 2009 happened, and his overall portfolio dropped nearly 50 percent in value. His resolve was challenged. "I should have listened to you," he told us, but he made his bed and he was going to lie in it…just not as comfortably as he had hoped. He made some lifestyle adjustments to reduce his portfolio withdrawals during the downturn in order to leave more of the portfolio in place to recover, and he is standing tall today. But now he maintains five years of stability and has never looked back.

"You might want to think about that going into it," I told her. After all, she had come to us with no stability at all and didn't even know it. I believe that was a real failure of her current advisor not to point that out. She is on board with our advice now, and I suspect she will be happy she built some stability when the next bear market comes.

Is five years of stability an absolute rule? Well, we think so. Why? Because we lived through the dot-com meltdown. We lived through 9/11. We lived through the Great Recession. We know how retirees react when they have no stability and watch their $1 million retirement account drop to $560,000 in a matter of months. It's not a happy place. Can you stomach a portfolio with only two or three years of stability in it? You might think you can, but you should think long and hard about your ability to stick to the investment plan when the next bear market comes.

## HOW IT WORKS

You need stability, and you need growth. Each is essential, and as we set up your retirement plan, you will have a bucket of money for each. In essence, your Stability Bucket is there to provide your immediate income for five years so that you will not find yourself in a position of having to dump stocks when they are temporarily selling at fire-sale prices.

Each year, after you have withdrawn from the Stability Bucket the amount that you agreed you would need, we take a look at both of those buckets and ask, "Where are we now?" If the Growth Bucket is way up, we can harvest some gains from those investments. We'll clip some from here, some from there, and we can use those gains to help replace the money that you withdrew from the Stability Bucket for income. If, however, the Growth Bucket is having a terrible year, then we might decide not to sell anything. Why sell when the price is down?

Here's how it works: Let's say you came to us with a million dollars and wanted to devise a retirement plan. After analyzing your situation and discussing in detail what your reasonable withdrawal rate would be, we would meet to talk about how it all would work.

**YOUR PORTFOLIO**

# $1,000,000

At the top of a whiteboard, I would write "$1,000,000." That's your retirement nest egg. I would explain that Social Security and other income streams are nice add-ons, but for our purposes we would just be looking at what that million-dollar portfolio was capable of doing for you.

**YOUR PORTFOLIO**

# $1,000,000

↓

Yearly withdrawal rate: **5%.**

**5% of $1,000,000 =**

**$50,000**

Below that figure, I would draw an arrow down and write the withdrawal rate that we had agreed upon—let's say it's the average of 5 percent. I'll draw another arrow down from there and write "$50,000." "That's what a 5 percent withdrawal rate will provide annually," I explain. "Are you still all right with that?"

"Yes, we can live on $50,000 a year plus Social Security," you might say.

"Okay, great," I say. "Now let's take out your next five years of plan withdrawals." I'll circle the $50,000 amount and write "times five" next to it. Then I'll draw two arrows, one to the left and one to the right. To the left I will write "$250,000" and label at as "Stability Bucket." To the right, I will write "Growth Bucket" and the amount remaining of their nest egg—that is, $750,000.

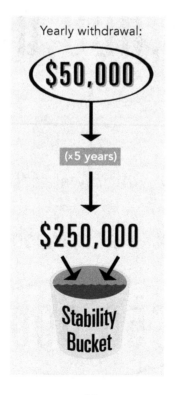

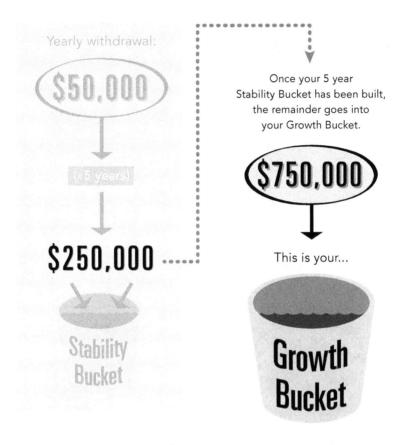

"You're going to get your retirement income from that Stability Bucket on the left," I explain. "And that bucket on the right, your Growth Bucket, is going to replenish your Stability Bucket every year that it makes sense to do so.

I draw a red arrow going out the bottom of the Stability Bucket showing one year's $50,000 income withdrawal. "Think of this as a leak in the bucket as you get your checks each month," I say. "Your Stability Bucket now only has $200,000 in it because you took $50,000 out. So what will we do to fix that leak? You need to keep that bucket filled up for five years, so where is that money going to come from to replenish it?"

"From the Growth Bucket," you would reply, and I will draw a green arrow from the Growth Bucket going into the top of the Stability Bucket.

**ONE YEAR LATER...**

$250,000

Stability Bucket

-$50,000

You withdrew $50,000 during the year, leaving a **Stability Bucket** value of...

$200,000

Your **Growth Bucket** may have grown from...

$750,000

$820,000

HOWEVER...

Growth Bucket

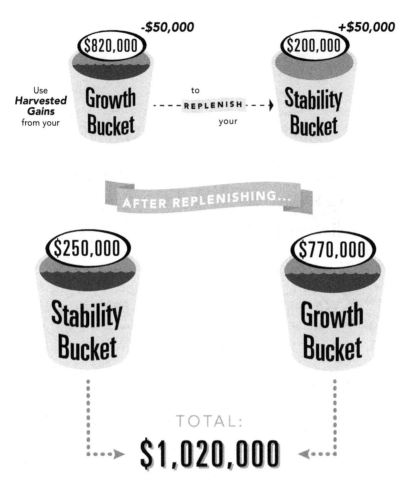

Despite withdrawing $50,000 from your portfolio,
your portfolio has grown and you have refilled your Stability Bucket.

"As you can see, it's a cycle. We've got money leaking out of the bottom of the Stability Bucket, and then we've got money coming back in if it was a good year." Then I explain what happens in the bad years. "Using this approach," I say, "you conceivably might have gotten, in 2008 and 2009, a monthly statement from us showing that the $750,000 you had put in your Growth Bucket suddenly only had $670,000 in there."

ONE YEAR LATER...

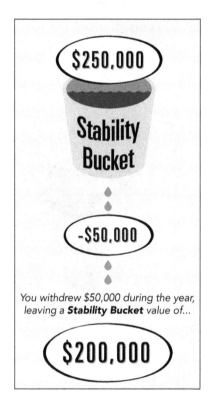

That might startle you. "Yes, it was a really bad correction," I explain. "But all that time, your Stability Bucket was there for you as you took out the withdrawals. In those years, we might not have had this green arrow from the Growth Bucket for two years or two and a half. We didn't take any money out of the Growth Bucket—why would we sell when those investments are just ridiculously on sale?

"So we just waited," I say. "A year went by, and the $250,000 that was in the Stability Bucket went down to $200,000. A second year went by, and you were down to $150,000. But there are three more years to go. At that point we were getting some gains to harvest from the Growth Bucket, and so we started refilling your Stability Bucket."

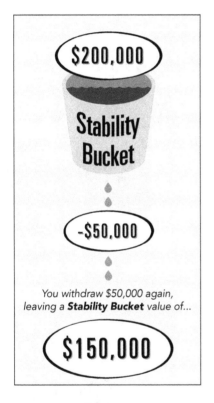

**$200,000**

**Stability Bucket**

**-$50,000**

*You withdraw $50,000 again, leaving a Stability Bucket value of...*

**$150,000**

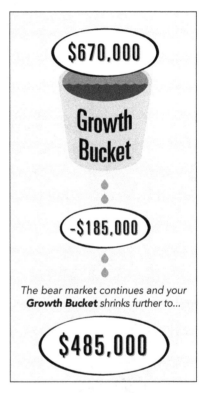

**$670,000**

**Growth Bucket**

**-$185,000**

*The bear market continues and your Growth Bucket shrinks further to...*

**$485,000**

**BUT THE NEXT YEAR...**

**$810,000**

The market recovers!
Your **Growth Bucket** refills
and reaches a value of...

**Growth Bucket**

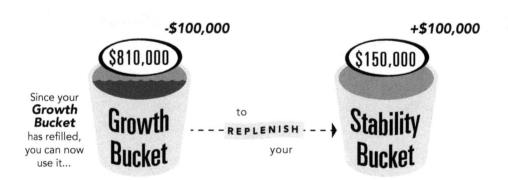

-$100,000

+$100,000

**$810,000**

**$150,000**

Since your **Growth Bucket** has refilled, you can now use it...

**Growth Bucket**

to
- - - **REPLENISH** - - →
your

**Stability Bucket**

AFTER REPLENISHING...

$250,000
Stability Bucket

$710,000
Growth Bucket

TOTAL:
$960,000

Despite a severe downturn, you've recovered nearly your entire portfolio. As the market continues to improve, your portfolio could expand well beyond the initial investment.

Our goal is to refill that Stability Bucket every year, if market conditions allow. When markets are good, there are usually plenty of gains to harvest. When markets are bad, we can afford to be patient. Understanding the mechanics of refilling your Stability Bucket, and having the discipline to follow through, is vital to your retirement success.

## WHY IT'S SO IMPORTANT

When you're not working anymore, and you have no plans to go back to work and you don't want to change your lifestyle, you need predictable cash flow—and that is why we built the approach the way we did.

It comes down to a fundamental of money management: You don't want to be withdrawing money from a fluctuating account in a down market. When you sell in a down market, either out of panic or out of necessity, you are locking in your losses.

You never can be sure what lies immediately ahead once you take that step into retirement, but bear markets do come with some regularity and are perfectly normal. Going back to World War II, there have now been 14 bear markets in the past 70 years, or about one every five years. Those bear markets had declines as small as 19 percent and as large as 57 percent, with the average being 31 percent. The average length of time it took to recover from the bear market was 3.3 years. So roughly speaking *it is perfectly normal for a retiree to see a 30 percent drop in their portfolio every five years and that it will take three years for the portfolio to recover from it!* [2]

It's not an uninterrupted run to prosperity. You can expect ups and downs. Still, some people are stunned when the bear comes around. "We should have seen this coming!" they say, but you cannot predict exactly. You just know it will happen, so you need to get ready.

---

2 J.P. Morgan Asset Management, Guide to the Markets, 2Q 2015 and Mark Hulbert, "Don't Fear the Bear", Wall Street Journal, March 7, 2014

As we have preached for years, portfolios should be built in anticipation of volatility, not in reaction to it. That is why we continue to stress our *Power of 5 Investing* philosophy. We build a five-year volatility cushion into our Stability Bucket, thereby allowing retirees to get through the inevitable market declines they will face. We know the declines are temporary, but the long-term upward march of the market has been a mainstay in the past. Staying appropriately invested in the market at all times provides the long-term growth potential our clients need to help them maintain their vision toward a comfortable lifestyle.

Those gyrations won't bother you as much if you have a Stability Bucket you can depend on for five years, whether the market is rising, falling, or in the doldrums. It's reassuring to know you have a plan. We track this for you so you know at all times exactly how many dollars are in your Stability Bucket and how many years that will last.

We're prepared to discuss the status of those numbers and what you would need going forward. Regardless of any crisis at hand, I can say: "We've got you covered. You'll be okay, and we're going to get through this." That's the power of the Stability Bucket.

## "WINTER IS COMING"

At the risk of dating this book, let me say I thoroughly enjoy the television series *Game of Thrones*, in which the characters are ominously reminded "winter is coming." Some of the characters have the foresight to prepare for the hardships they will face; those who don't suffer badly.

The certainty of economic cycles is not that we can time them but that we know they will come and how often they have come historically. People who retire today could see many more bear markets in their lifetime. That's why the Stability Bucket is a pillar of *Power of 5 Investing*. Portfolios should be built in anticipation of volatility, not in response to it.

Our approach is rooted in our own experience of how people feel in good times and bad. The emotions surrounding money are powerful. You might intellectually understand what is happening in a downturn but still feel a churning in your gut—and those emotions cannot be ignored. The Stability and Growth Buckets are a disciplined approach to taking the emotion out of retirement investing. We offer the reassurance that you will be all right. I have found it gratifying that clients, at their annual review meetings, have been so well versed in what we have taught them about these principles. It has become central to their way of thinking about their retirement path.

Make no mistake: Winter is coming. Will you be ready?

# CHAPTER 4

## THE *FIVE PERCENT* LIMIT

M any of our clients are affiliated with Procter & Gamble, head-quartered in Cincinnati. P&G is a venerable old company, founded in 1837. I worked there briefly, and my wife worked there for many years. I have a deep respect for it.

Many employees had looked to the company profit-sharing plan as their means to a comfortable retirement. In a good year, which was almost every year, the company added money to each employee's retirement account. For many years there was no option for employees to make their own contributions; it was purely profit sharing, and it worked out so well for so long that employees had no reason to make additional retirement contributions.

This was not a pension. There were no guarantees. And every dollar contributed to the retirement account was invested in Procter & Gamble stock. It was a fantastic deal for those who worked there for thirty years, as many of our clients did—as long as it was the right thirty years. People who had been making $60,000 a year could walk out with a million and a half dollars in their retirement account, most of which was provided by the company's contributions. P&G made many people's retirement secure. It was a blessing for them.

Many of those accounts, however, remained 100 percent invested in P&G stock. Even after the Enron debacle, when employees gained some limited ability to diversify away from company stock due to government mandates, many people didn't seem to get around to doing so. "The company has treated me well," they told themselves. "The stock goes up and it goes down, but over time it has done really well."

And that was true for a long time. Except for this past decade.

In January of 2000, the US economy was growing, and jobs were plentiful. Procter & Gamble named a new CEO the year before, and he had an ambitious plan to continue aggressively growing the company. The stock price peaked at about $117 a share, and everyone was pleased.

And then the company tried an acquisition of a large consumer products company. It didn't go well, and the deal fell apart. And within three months, P&G's stock dropped more than 50 percent even as the broader stock market continued notching gains. Wall Street had lost confidence in P&G, and many employees had lost half their retirement dollars in the blink of an eye.

There were employees in their early 50s and younger who had been looking at their accounts with this stalwart American company and saw so much money in there that they were ready to retire or to move on to a second career.

"I told P&G that I was going to move on to a new phase in my life," one employee told me. He was 48 at the time. "I had other things I wanted to do. I had more in my retirement account than I ever imagined, so I gave notice. I was out of there." And then the stock price took its dive, and he hadn't diversified. It was too late to get his job back. He didn't sleep well for a long time.

It happened to General Electric stock as well. "We invented the light bulb," the GE people said, "and the steam locomotive. We changed the world." Even so, that did not mean their retirement was going to be secure. At least P&G stock clawed its way back after the recession of 2008–2009. GE has not recovered. Its stock was hovering around $40 a share before the recession and fell as low as $7. As I write this, it still isn't much more than halfway back. GE employees are facing a lost decade, just like the P&G people did.

Bad things can happen to really good companies, and hardworking, loyal employees can have their retirements devastated by forces largely beyond their control. Your company's generous retirement contributions may have made you rich on paper while you were still working, but the game is how to remain financially comfortable after you retire. Placing all of your bets on one company, no matter how storied their reputation may be, is often a recipe for retirement failure. You need to diversify in retirement, if not sooner. Selling company stock is not a sign of disloyalty; it's evidence of common sense. Diversifying doesn't necessarily guarantee a profit or protect you against a loss, but it is a technique designed to avoid situations like these.

It's easy to forget or to think it can't happen to you, but make no mistake about it. Your dreams can be destroyed. There's a crucial lesson here, and it's about the importance of diversification.

## TWENTY TIMES AS MUCH COMFORT

Our rule is that no single growth investment should make up more than 5 percent of your portfolio. That's the level of diversification that we believe could provide you the comfort of knowing your portfolio will manage through good times and bad, whether for the economy or for a particular holding.

Our 5 percent rule means you are going to have twenty different holdings in your Growth Bucket. Why twenty? Classic studies of diversification by Benjamin Graham in his *The Intelligent Investor* and the landmark study "The Effect of Diversification on Risk" by W.H. Wagner and C.S. Lau indicate that somewhere between 10–30 holdings result in a significant reduction in company-specific risk. It doesn't vanish, but it really levels out. One particular holding should not be able to wreck the retirement portfolio.

The research assumes that if the market is up or down, those individual investments are not all moving the same way. They are said to be noncorrelated, meaning their returns do not move in lockstep with each other. The more you can build a portfolio of those noncorrelated investments, the better your portfolio's ability to smooth out the ride. As one zigs, another zags.

Note: Keep in mind that this discussion of the 5 percent limit applies only to the Growth Bucket, not to the Stability Bucket. The latter is the source of your annual income, so we take as little risk as possible in the Stability Bucket.

Investing during retirement is not supposed to be exciting (If you want your money to be exciting, go to Las Vegas. Just be sure to leave your serious money at home). If we do our jobs right, your retirement portfolio should be pretty boring. What you want to see is that check coming consistently. You want to deposit the same amount of money in the bank every month and feel good about the ride. You understand that risks are involved in investing, but at the same time you want to feel comfortable about it. Rather than a thrill, investment is supposed to be a means toward achieving your goals.

## TWO VIEWS OF DIVERSIFICATION

We look at diversification in two ways—*across* asset classes and *within* them.

The three major asset classes are stocks, bonds, and cash. You can divide your holdings *across* those classes for a level of diversification. In diversifying *across* asset classes, we may determine, for example, that 15 percent of your overall portfolio should be in large US stocks. Now, that's still a big portion of the portfolio, but we actually have several holdings making up that 15 percent.

You also need to diversify your holdings *within* an asset class. You can slice and dice them in a wide variety of ways. With stocks, for example, you have large, medium, and small companies, and you have international and domestic. Similarly, with bonds you have corporates, government, and international.

You might wonder why we would have such an array of stocks that are doing basically the same thing. It's because they're still large US stocks. Consider the traditional breakdown of value, blend, and growth. A value stock might be the classic solid manufacturing company that pays a good dividend. An exciting, rapidly expanding company would be a growth stock. A blend stock might demonstrate qualities of both value and growth stocks.

Even within those styles, you can find a lot of variety. One value manager might have a strong focus on finding large US companies that just pay solid dividends. Perhaps the stock price just plods along, but you're getting that valuable dividend all the time. Another value manager says, "I don't need to worry about dividends at all. I will look around for a beaten down firm with a possible turnaround, and I'll buy when it's cheap. I'll take a chance, and if they do turn it around, we'll make a killing on it."

In other words, different investment managers have their own approaches. For that reason, if 15 percent of your portfolio is in large US value stocks, we still want at least three or four holdings in that category. This ensures, at least at the start, that no single holding can violate the 5 percent rule.

## REBALANCING

Rebalancing is an important discipline in portfolio management. At least annually you should compare your current portfolio to your original investment plan and make sure the portfolio is still on track. Why is this important? Because a particular style often will go through a cycle of three, four, even five years when it is in vogue and has a great run. For example, for three years in the late 1990s, it seemed you could do no wrong in the tech space. The NASDAQ Composite climbed from around 1,300 in late 1997 to 5,048 in March of 2000, an incredible gain of 288 percent in a little over two years! But then, just a year later, it fell to 1,900 and eventually dropped to just above 1,200 in September of 2002. All of those spectacular gains achieved in two years were totally wiped out two and a half years later.

When a particular investment like tech stocks are flying high, you may be tempted to not rebalance, but if you don't, you will end up with a portfolio that is heavily weighted with the style that has been in favor. Maybe you start off at 20 percent, but soon it can become 50 percent as you keep riding that wave.

"I've got to have more tech," some clients were telling us back then. We told them they already owned an appropriate amount of tech stocks and as they rose in value we needed to sell some off and get back into some of the boring dividend payers. "Why would I do that?" they asked. "I could be making so much more money."

Or they could be losing so much more money. Anyone who didn't rebalance before the tech crash got punished badly. The Growth Bucket will have some pure growth stocks and some seemingly stodgy ones, but they all have their day in the sun. We try to keep the appropriate mix. You have to have the discipline to rebalance.

You might think of it as taking some of your chips off the table. I don't like gambling, but it illustrates the principle. If you're in Vegas and you run a hundred dollars up to $250, you might decide to lock in that gain by putting your winnings in your pocket. You'll keep playing with your original hundred dollars, but you have decided that's as far as you are going to go. It can be hard to muster that discipline, though, when you're on a winning streak.

In investing, too, discipline isn't easy when times are good. It's difficult for some clients to accept that we're telling them to sell off part of an investment that's done really well and put the money into a holding that seems sluggish. And again, we monitor the investment managers we use. If one is falling too far behind his peers, we take action. We fire those who don't meet expectations.

Investors might start off diversified, but they tend to take their eye off the ball. People often tell us they put money into a fund long ago but haven't looked at it since. It can be good to leave your investments alone, but doing so should be a deliberate choice with regular reviews to ensure the investments you have chosen are still aligned with your goals.

Diversification and its cousin, rebalancing, are vital tools to retirement success. Ignore them, and you will find yourself whipsawed by a downturn in the markets. Be disciplined about both of them and your portfolio could thank you.

# CHAPTER 5

## *FIVE WORDS* OF WISDOM

Most of us remember exactly where we were the morning of September 11, 2001. That horrific day not only changed the lives of thousands of families in New York; it also set our country on a complicated path whose outcomes and implications are still being debated. We truly will never forget.

Not quite as many people will remember where they were just seven years later, on September 15, 2008. I will never forget it. Over the prior weeks, I had been following the story that Lehman Brothers, one of the most venerable financial institutions in US history, was seeking additional capital and a potential sale of itself to a foreign firm. That a proud American institution like Lehman was seeking help was shocking enough. But when I arrived in the office early that Monday morning, I was simply stunned. Lehman had not found any willing buyer on the entire planet and was forced to file for bankruptcy. Even worse, Lehman had sought support from the federal government and was denied. "Too big to fail" was not part of the vocabulary at that time.

At its peak, Lehman employed more than 26,000 people. This would be far and away the largest bankruptcy the United States had ever seen. The US stock market, which had started falling almost 12 months earlier, plunged on September 15. Although we didn't know it at the time, we were headed for some very dark days. Before it was all over, the Standard & Poor's 500 Index would fall nearly 57 percent from its record high, hitting bottom at 676 on March 9, 2009. On that same day, The Dow Jones Industrial Average would close at 6507, a 54 percent drop from its record high. The collapse of Lehman precipitated one of the worst financial market crises since the 1930s.

And so investors' portfolios collapsed and never recovered, right? That is certainly the picture painted by the mainstream media. They're not about to let a perfectly good crisis go to waste. The media's guiding principle seems to be if it bleeds, it leads—and there was plenty of bleeding to talk about back then. Despite evidence to the contrary, the media still see blood everywhere they look these days.

We are now several years removed from those dark days. It may have seemed to some that this time was certainly different, that we would never find our way back to prosperity. And what have we learned? *It's never different this time.* Those are the five words of wisdom that constitute the fifth principle of *Power of 5 Investing*.

Our clients, following our approach, were able to persevere through the downturn from their patience and faith. Our approach has been battle tested once again, just as it was during the terrorist attacks, the dot-com meltdown, the Long-Term Capital Management crisis, and other challenges.

History may not always exactly repeat itself, but it sure does rhyme. We will be tested again. We know the bears will come, but we do not pretend to know when, and we certainly will not abandon stocks before, during, or after such a market. Market timing is a fool's game.

Instead, we continue to work with clients to make a plan, and we help them stick to it. Our *Power of 5 Investing* principles will guide us, through good times and bad—and in the midst of the latter, we can be confident that we are on the way back toward the former.

## THE PREMISE OF THE POWER

Our fundamental belief is that it is never different this time. Our longtime clients, going back a decade or two, could have cried that the sky was falling on any number of occasions—and sometimes that is what seemed to be happening

The reassuring answer comes in actual client experience. Consider people who retired in the mid-1990s. Think of the distressing events in the news since then. In the late '90s, portfolios were booming during the run-up of the dot-coms and tech stocks. Then came the tech stock meltdown and the 9/11 attacks. Later in the decade came the housing market crisis and those recessionary upheavals as the economy contracted and jobs vanished. We saw some truly troubling times. But where are those retirees today? If they had a sound plan and followed it, they were able to withdraw income regularly, and they still have more money today than when they started their retirement.

Remember those five words of wisdom: it's never different this time. Things will turn out all right, even though it might not feel that way when we are enduring the crisis du jour.

## IT JUST KEEPS GETTING BETTER. REALLY. IT'S NOT AS BAD AS YOU THINK.

It seems sometimes that we go out of our way to find things to worry about. Yet the truth is that for the majority of people, things pretty much are better than ever before in the history of the planet. Whenever I hear talk about how bad things have become, I understand that, yes, some people are hurting and need our help, but the vast majority of Americans wake up each day with a roof over our heads, clean water, and more than enough to eat.

What we need is a healthy dose of gratitude for how great things are today. How soon, as a society, do we forget the trials faced by those who went before us? There are still plenty of people alive who recall the depths of the Great Depression, the food rationing of the Second World War, and the atrocities of a world in turmoil.

The comedian Louis C.K. has this tremendously insightful bit he does called "Everything is Amazing and Nobody is Happy." He describes the incredulity of Americans whose cell phones don't download data the instant they touch the screen or who are delayed

20 minutes on a cross-country flight. They seem to have no perspective on the remarkable efforts needed to create such prosperity.

My grandfather lived through the Depression and spent most of his working years in a bus factory. Once at the dinner table, he saw me cutting the fat off a pork chop. He speared it off my plate with his fork, cut it up, and ate it. "It's good," he said. "We would never have thought of throwing that away back in the day. We didn't know if we'd have enough to eat the next day." The fat equaled calories, and calories meant energy. Nothing was wasted. Fast forward to today, and my kids will cut off the tiniest, nearly invisible sliver of fat that remains on any meat on their plates. I tell them the story about my grandfather and the pork fat, and they think I'm kidding. Fortunately, my grandfather's lessons about the value of a dollar left an impression on me, and I try to share those lessons with my own children.

We could do with more of his resourceful attitude. It seems so many people feel a sense of entitlement these days. We need to get back on track with both personal responsibility and corporate responsibility.

Today's challenges are real, but they are hardly worse than what we have managed to endure. We came through our troubles then, and we thrived. We always come through strong and full of promise. Such is the cycle of humanity.

And such is the cycle of the markets. The fifth principle of *Power of 5 Investing* is not just that it's never different this time. Underlying all of this is a fundamental belief that things always get better.

That is the premise upon which the other principles are built. It's the premise that makes all the planning possible.

The human spirit can be stifled by oppression and bureaucracy, but it cannot be defeated forever. Things are getting better, despite all the whining and handwringing by the mainstream media and big government. Let the dreamers and innovators thrive, and things will get better.

If you believe that America and the capitalist system is broken and that we're never going to be able to invent and improve things that make the world a better place, then you shouldn't be investing in stocks. This doom and gloom rhetoric not only ignores the historical record, but it cannot be a fun way to live. Rest assured: I believe we will work our way out of our problems. The world moves on, and things get better. You can count on it.

I am an unabashed optimist on the future of America. Human beings are creative and innovative with an ambition to reach for the bigger and the better. We have the ability to outgrow every problem. We'll be okay.

Those who likewise trust the power of our potential will understand the foundation of *Power of 5 Investing*. No secret financial fad here. These are fundamentals, tested by time and experience, unadorned and far more powerful than any fad you might find. These principles are set up to keep on working through good times and through bad times, on a trajectory trending ever upward over time. If you believe that, and if you set aside enough reserves to get you through any rough patch while your nest egg grows, you will be well on your way toward retirement prosperity.

# CHAPTER 6

## POWER OF 5 INVESTING® IN ACTION

In this chapter, we will take a practical look at those five principles of *Power of 5 Investing*. I want you to see our principles in action as they would be experienced by a typical client.

### IMPLEMENTING PRINCIPLE NUMBER ONE—FIVE STEPS OF INVESTING

Joe and Jane Smith are both 62 years old. He has been considering retiring after 34 years of increasing responsibility at a large manufacturing company, where he has accumulated $1 million in his company's retirement plan through a combination of his own saving and generous company contributions.

Their Social Security is expected to contribute $24,000 per year of inflation-adjusted income, and they are planning to begin taking those benefits right away.

Joe has access to an employer-sponsored health-care plan for retirees that will continue his health insurance until he is eligible for Medicare at age 65. They plan to stay in their home, which should be paid off in ten years or so. They have some modest tax deductions for home mortgage interest, property taxes, and charitable contributions, making their effective combined federal and state tax rate about 20 percent. Their children are grown and not financially dependent on them.

This is the planning phase of the relationship. In this phase we need to learn all we can about the client's goals and needs, their time horizon, their risk tolerance, and the resources available to them to achieve their goals. We examined that process in chapter 1. This is the phase where we get to know the couple, document their financial affairs, and prepare to begin.

## IMPLEMENTING PRINCIPLE NUMBER TWO—LIVING ON FIVE PERCENT

In this phase we start talking real numbers. Joe's final salary was $80,000 before taxes, retirement plan contributions, and benefits costs. The Smith's had heard that you only need 80 percent of your salary when you retire, but we advise them that most people seem to spend about the same amount of money in retirement as they did while working—they just spend it on different things. After some back and forth, we estimate they will need about $64,000 in their pockets ($5,333/month after taxes) to feel comfortable. This will be provided by

- Social Security at $2,000/month—no taxes withheld

- IRA withdrawals of $3,333/month—$4,167/month minus taxes at 20 percent. Federal and state taxes are withheld and are sent in.

- Total cash in client's pocket: $5,333/month ($2,000 + $3,333)

The $4,167/month withdrawal from the IRA represents $50,000 of annual withdrawals. On a $1 million portfolio, this is an effective withdrawal rate of 5 percent. In reviewing the Smith's living needs, health situation, and family longevity, we determine that a 5 percent portfolio withdrawal rate seems appropriate here.

The couple plans to keep this $50,000 annual withdrawal level during their retirement years (i.e., they are not going to take automatic raises for inflation). Instead they will call in and ask for a special onetime IRA withdrawal should an emergency situation arise.

## IMPLEMENTING PRINCIPLE NUMBER THREE—FIVE YEARS OF STABILITY

I meet with the Smith's to explain the Stability and Growth Buckets (diagramming them on a whiteboard as I explained in chapter 3). I write down their annual income needs and multiply that by five to determine the amount they need to set aside for stability. I explain to them that the remainder will be invested for growth.

For this couple, who will be withdrawing $50,000 a year, we set aside $250,000 as an appropriate amount in their Stability Bucket. The remaining $750,000 will be invested toward the potential for longer-term growth.

## IMPLEMENTING PRINCIPLE NUMBER FOUR—THE FIVE PERCENT LIMIT

Let's take a look at a sample investment proposal that we might develop for the Smith's.

In keeping with our policy that no single growth holding should constitute more than 5 percent of the couple's portfolio, we begin distributing their money into various investment vehicles.

In this particular case, the investment vehicle for the couple's Stability Bucket was a money market fund. The remaining $750,000 is invested with a focus on growth potential in our "Growth Bucket". The Growth Bucket is made up of numerous asset classes like large-cap value, emerging markets, high-yield bonds, etc. Each of those asset classes has a target value, which we then proceed to fill by having the client buy various investments.

We use multiple investments, even within the same asset class, to achieve diversification for the client. In most cases we try to stay pretty far away from the 5 percent diversification limit.

## PROPOSED ACTIONS

Prepared for Joe and Jane Smith

| | CURRENT | | ACTION | PROPOSED | |
|---|---|---|---|---|---|
| | MARKET VALUE | % OF PORTFOLIO | | MARKET VALUE | % OF PORTFOLIO |
| MONEY MARKET FUND IRA | $1,000,000 | 100.00% | SELL $750,000 | $250,000 | 25.00% |
| STABILITY BUCKET TOTAL | $1,000,000 | 100.00% | | $250,000 5 Years | 25.00% |
| Target Portfolio | | 100.00% | | $250,000 | 25.00% |
| Difference | | | | $0 | 0.00% |

### LARGE CAP VALUE

| | CURRENT | | ACTION | PROPOSED | |
|---|---|---|---|---|---|
| | MARKET VALUE | % OF PORTFOLIO | | MARKET VALUE | % OF PORTFOLIO |
| LARGE CAP VALUE IRA | - | - | BUY $23,800 | $23,800 | 2.38% |
| LARGE CAP VALUE IRA | - | - | BUY $23,800 | $23,800 | 2.38% |
| LARGE CAP VALUE IRA | - | - | BUY $23,800 | $23,800 | 2.38% |
| LARGE CAP VALUE IRA | - | - | BUY $23,800 | $23,800 | 2.38% |
| LARGE CAP VALUE IRA | - | - | BUY $23,800 | $23,800 | 2.38% |
| LARGE CAP VALUE TOTAL | $0 | | | $119,000 | 11.90% |
| Target Portfolio | | 0.00% | | $119,000 | 11.90% |
| Difference | | | | $0 | 0.00% |

## CURRENT

## PROPOSED

### LARGE CAP BLEND

| | MARKET VALUE | % OF PORTFOLIO | ACTION | MARKET VALUE | % OF PORTFOLIO |
|---|---|---|---|---|---|
| LARGE CAP BLEND FUND #1 \| IRA | - | - | BUY $21,600 | $21,600 | 2.16% |
| LARGE CAP BLEND FUND #2 \| IRA | - | - | BUY $21,600 | $21,600 | 2.16% |
| LARGE CAP BLEND FUND #3 \| IRA | - | - | BUY $21,600 | $21,600 | 2.16% |
| LARGE CAP BLEND FUND #4 \| IRA | - | - | BUY $21,600 | $21,600 | 2.16% |
| LARGE CAP BLEND FUND #5 \| IRA | - | - | BUY $21,600 | $21,600 | 2.16% |
| LARGE CAP BLEND TOTAL | $0 | 0.00% | | $108,000 | 10.80% |
| Target Portfolio | | | | $108,000 | 10.80% |
| Difference | | | | $0 | 0.00% |

### LARGE CAP GROWTH

| | MARKET VALUE | % OF PORTFOLIO | ACTION | MARKET VALUE | % OF PORTFOLIO |
|---|---|---|---|---|---|
| LARGE CAP GROWTH FUND #1 \| IRA | - | - | BUY $19,400 | $19,400 | 1.94% |
| LARGE CAP GROWTH FUND #2 \| IRA | - | - | BUY $19,400 | $19,400 | 1.94% |
| LARGE CAP GROWTH FUND #3 \| IRA | - | - | BUY $19,400 | $19,400 | 1.94% |
| LARGE CAP GROWTH FUND #4 \| IRA | - | - | BUY $19,400 | $19,400 | 1.94% |
| LARGE CAP GROWTH FUND #5 \| IRA | - | - | BUY $19,400 | $19,400 | 1.94% |
| LARGE CAP GROWTH TOTAL | $0 | 0.00% | | $97,000 | 9.70% |
| Target Portfolio | | | | $97,000 | 9.70% |
| Difference | | | | $0 | 0.00% |

## CURRENT

| | MARKET VALUE | % OF PORTFOLIO |
|---|---|---|

## PROPOSED

| | ACTION | MARKET VALUE | % OF PORTFOLIO |
|---|---|---|---|

### SMALL/MID VALUE

| | CURRENT MARKET VALUE | CURRENT % OF PORTFOLIO | ACTION | PROPOSED MARKET VALUE | PROPOSED % OF PORTFOLIO |
|---|---|---|---|---|---|
| SMALL/MID VALUE FUND #1 IRA | - | | BUY $14,000 | $14,000 | 1.40% |
| SMALL/MID VALUE FUND #2 IRA | - | | BUY $21,000 | $21,000 | 2.10% |
| SMALL/MID VALUE TOTAL | $0 | 0.00% | | $35,000 | 3.50% |
| Target Portfolio | | | | $35,000 | 3.50% |
| Difference | | | | $0 | 0.00% |

### SMALL/MID BLEND

| | CURRENT MARKET VALUE | CURRENT % OF PORTFOLIO | ACTION | PROPOSED MARKET VALUE | PROPOSED % OF PORTFOLIO |
|---|---|---|---|---|---|
| SMALL/MID BLEND FUND #1 IRA | - | | BUY $19,000 | $19,000 | 1.90% |
| SMALL/MID BLEND FUND #2 IRA | - | | BUY $13,000 | $13,000 | 1.30% |
| SMALL/MID BLEND TOTAL | $0 | 0.00% | | $32,000 | 3.20% |
| Target Portfolio | | | | $32,000 | 3.20% |
| Difference | | | | $0 | 0.00% |

### SMALL/MID GROWTH

| | CURRENT MARKET VALUE | CURRENT % OF PORTFOLIO | ACTION | PROPOSED MARKET VALUE | PROPOSED % OF PORTFOLIO |
|---|---|---|---|---|---|
| SMALL/MID GROWTH FUND #1 IRA | - | | BUY $17,000 | $17,000 | 1.70% |
| SMALL/MID GROWTH FUND #2 IRA | - | | BUY $12,000 | $12,000 | 1.20% |
| SMALL/MID GROWTH TOTAL | $0 | 0.00% | | $29,000 | 2.90% |
| Target Portfolio | | | | $29,000 | 2.90% |
| Difference | | | | $0 | 0.00% |

## CURRENT | | | PROPOSED |

### INTERNATIONAL

| | MARKET VALUE | % OF PORTFOLIO | ACTION | MARKET VALUE | % OF PORTFOLIO |
|---|---|---|---|---|---|
| INTERNATIONAL FUND #1 \| IRA | - | - | BUY $30,000 | $30,000 | 3.00% |
| INTERNATIONAL FUND #2 \| IRA | - | - | BUY $30,000 | $30,000 | 3.00% |
| INTERNATIONAL FUND #3 \| IRA | - | - | BUY $30,000 | $30,000 | 3.00% |
| INTERNATIONAL FUND #4 \| IRA | - | - | BUY $30,000 | $30,000 | 3.00% |
| INTERNATIONAL FUND #5 \| IRA | - | - | BUY $30,000 | $30,000 | 3.00% |
| INTERNATIONAL FUND #6 \| IRA | - | - | BUY $30,000 | $30,000 | 3.00% |
| INTERNATIONAL TOTAL | $0 | 0.00% | | $180,000 | 18.00% |
| Target Portfolio | | | | $180,000 | 18.00% |
| Difference | | | | $0 | 0.00% |

### EMERGING MARKETS

| | MARKET VALUE | % OF PORTFOLIO | ACTION | MARKET VALUE | % OF PORTFOLIO |
|---|---|---|---|---|---|
| EMERGING MARKETS FUND #1 \| IRA | - | - | BUY $30,000 | $30,000 | 3.00% |
| EMERGING MARKETS FUND #2 \| IRA | - | - | BUY $20,000 | $20,000 | 2.00% |
| EMERGING MARKETS TOTAL | $0 | 0.00% | | $50,000 | 5.00% |
| Target Portfolio | | | | $50,000 | 5.00% |
| Difference | | | | $0 | 0.00% |

## CURRENT | | PROPOSED

| | MARKET VALUE | % OF PORTFOLIO | ACTION | MARKET VALUE | % OF PORTFOLIO |
|---|---|---|---|---|---|
| **INVESTMENT GRADE BONDS** | | | | | |
| INVESTMENT GRADE BONDS FUND | IRA | - | | BUY $50,000 | $50,000 | 5.00% |
| INVESTMENT GRADE BONDS TOTAL | $0 | 0.00% | | $50,000 | 5.00% |
| **Target Portfolio** | | | | $50,000 | 5.00% |
| **Difference** | | | | $0 | 0.00% |
| **INTERNATIONAL BOND** | | | | | |
| INTERNATIONAL BOND FUND | IRA | - | | BUY $25,000 | $25,000 | 2.50% |
| INTERNATIONAL BOND TOTAL | $0 | 0.00% | | $25,000 | 2.50% |
| **Target Portfolio** | | | | $25,000 | 2.50% |
| **Difference** | | | | $0 | 0.00% |
| **HIGH YIELD BOND** | | | | | |
| HIGH YIELD BOND FUND | IRA | - | | BUY $25,000 | $25,000 | 2.50% |
| HIGH YIELD BOND TOTAL | $0 | 0.00% | | $25,000 | 2.50% |
| **Target Portfolio** | | | | $25,000 | 2.50% |
| **Difference** | | | | $0 | 0.00% |
| **PORTFOLIO TOTALS** | $1,000,000 | 100.00% | | $1,000,000 | 100.00% |

# IMPLEMENTING PRINCIPLE NUMBER FIVE—FIVE WORDS OF WISDOM

We reinforce *Power of 5 Investing* with the Smith's by making sure they understand the underlying principle that drives all the others: Things will get better. This time it will not be an exception to the rule. We emphasize those five words of wisdom: *it's never different this time.*

The market recovers. The economy recovers. Yes, it has its peaks and valleys, and past performance is not a guarantee with bear markets coming regularly, but the historical evidence shows that when the bull returns it pulls the market generally higher over the years.

That's why it is essential to separate your income needs for five years into a Stability Bucket—so that you can ride those waves in the stock market and eventually capture that growth, without having to let your growth holdings go when they are on sale. Persevere and you will prosper.

Each year we will meet with the Smith's for their annual review, making sure we return to Principle Number One, the five steps of investing. The annual review is a great opportunity to revisit their goals and plans, making any adjustments as necessary to keep them on track. With *Power of 5 Investing*, the Smith's are well on their way toward their vision of retirement success!

# CHAPTER 7

## READY FOR THE RISKS

**"** I probably need a psychiatrist more than a financial advisor," the retired widow told me with a smile. We had discussed her financial situation at length, and I had given her my assessment of the biggest risk that she was facing.

She was 74 but had only recently retired, and she was quite conversant on market matters. She told me that in the 2008–2009 crash, she had held on to her stocks, but then as the Dow began rising again, she began selling them off at various stages in the recovery. She had been totally out of stocks for some time, even as the market continued its tremendous climb. She had converted it all to cash and still had $1.5 million.

She had been seeking advice about the right time to get back into the market. She had worried when stock prices were low; now she was worried that they were too high and she would be buying just before a correction. She was, frankly, in a state of "analysis paralysis."

She said she needed time to think about our recommendations and perhaps would do something the next year. I asked a few questions to get at why she continued to hesitate to make a decision. She had a laundry list of reasons not to get back into the market right now.

- The market was at all-time highs.
- The Fed was interfering with interest rates too much.
- Even if the markets were bad, she would still have to pay the advisor's fee.
- She had five proposals from five advisors in neat little piles and needed time to study them.

So what was my response? I told her to throw away all of the proposals, including mine. She seemed shocked by this and asked why I would say such a thing, especially since I had clearly put so much time into our proposal for her.

I explained that all of the investment plans in the world would be worthless to her because she failed to recognize the single greatest threat to her retirement—*inflation*—and its associated loss of purchasing power.

# INFLATION RISK

Inflation has always been, and always will be, the number-one threat to a successful retirement. And the only proven way to combat this risk is to have a healthy dose of stocks in your portfolio to provide the potential for longer-term growth needed to outpace inflation. I proceeded to explain this to her.

"You are right about my fee," I told her. "It is like a constant leak in the bucket, always taking away 1 percent of your portfolio. And you feel it because we very clearly disclose the fee and show it being deducted from your account every quarter. Inflation is a lot like that, except it will be a 3 or 4 percent fee—and it is hidden. It just keeps eating away at you, year after year, and you don't realize it until it's too late to do anything about it."

I asked her to imagine she was stuffing her $1.5 million in her mattress, then going to sleep for twenty years like Rip Van Winkle. "With inflation at the average of around 3.5 percent," I asked, "how much do you think you would have when you woke up?"

She answered, of course, $1.5 million. But with the effects of inflation, that $1.5 million wouldn't even buy half as much stuff as it did 20 years earlier. That's how awful inflation is for retirees. I then asked her if she felt like she could live on half of what she had, because she had put herself on exactly that path. Her indecision and inaction will cost her half of her wealth.

She said nobody had ever put it like that to her before.

She doesn't understand the enemy yet. It is attacking her right now, and she doesn't even feel it. Until she does, I can't help her. If she ever comes around, we'll have a plan ready to help her.

There are a lot of risks to retirees, but inflation matters immensely. It is hard for people to grasp that importance, since its effects are so insidious and slow. You have to plan to deal with inflation early on, before you get hammered. Inflation is the biggest risk that retirees face (except for one more that I often see, which I will explain at the end of this chapter).

Now let's take a look at the range of other threats, such as market risk and health-care concerns and taxes and even the prospect that you will live too long. They're the more popular ones to talk about—but just keep in mind that lurking behind all of them is the specter of inflation.

## MARKET RISK

In the booming years of the late 1990s, I saw office workers who would secretly day-trade from their desks, caught up in the excitement. They chased what was hot. And after the recession of 2008–2009, I saw people run screaming from any type of market risk whatsoever, even as stocks were selling at fire-sale valuations unlike anything we had seen in decades. They say fear and greed are the two greatest drivers of the markets. We've seen plenty of both in the last twenty years.

Market risk is normally thought of as the risk of having your retirement exposed to the volatility of stocks. It clearly is the risk that people want to talk about the most, and it's the one that the media are going to hype. More books are written about it and bad advice dispensed about it than any other risk that retirees face.

Retirees get the impression that they must stay away from this risk—and that's utterly untrue. You need the markets for growth so that you can beat inflation, and historically the only way to do that consistently over time has been to own high-quality stocks. Whether that means individual stocks or mutual funds isn't the point. We have to have a reliable weapon against inflation.

That's why you need to have exposure to the equity markets at all times and in an appropriate amount. Here's some of the bad advice that you will commonly hear:

- *Don't own stocks in retirement, they're too dangerous. You should own bonds instead because at least you're guaranteed to get your principal back.* That can be true. With US Treasuries, you will get your principal back as long as you hold the instrument to maturity. But if the interest paid on that Treasury security does not exceed the rate of inflation, you will actually lose purchasing power over the life of the investment. The only thing guaranteed here was the loss of purchasing power of the principal. Sounds like a bad retirement plan to me.

- *If you do want to own stocks, they should never make up a higher percentage of your portfolio than 100 minus your age.* According to that "Rule of 100," a 60-year-old, for example, shouldn't have any more than 40 percent in stocks. And a 30-year-old should limit stocks to 70 percent of their portfolio. Perhaps this rule of thumb should be renamed the "Rule of Stupid Retirement Investing." Our advice? Retirees need to hold anywhere from 50–85 percent of their portfolios in stocks at all times. For younger clients still accumulating for retirement, the guidance is closer to 80–90 percent stocks, with a few noncorrelated fixed income holdings added for diversification.

- *Only put as much money into stocks as you are comfortable losing.* The presumption here is that anything you put in the stock market is probably going to get lost so be prepared to survive on what you have left. That is a fear-based attitude, and you can overcome it by understanding how the markets help us.

These views of market risk have it all backward. The real definition of market risk should be the risk that retirees face from not being in the market at all. They lose the opportunity to outpace inflation and grow their wealth enough to sustain a 30-year retirement.

*Power of 5 Investing* doesn't eliminate market risk. Instead it leverages the power of stocks to help you achieve your retirement goals.

## HEALTH-CARE RISK

Health-care costs are clearly a significant issue for retirees and potentially a major threat to a secure retirement. According to the 2014 Fidelity Benefits Consulting study "Retiree Health Costs Hold Steady," a 65-year-old couple retiring in 2014 will need an average of $220,000 (in today's dollars) to cover medical expenses throughout retirement. That's pretty scary.

With longevity increasing so dramatically, many people are now living to advanced ages with conditions that would have killed us in previous generations. This is leading to an explosion in elder care expenses or what people used to refer to as nursing home care.

Today's retirees, at least the ones we work with, generally don't want anything to do with nursing homes. If they reach a stage where assistance is needed with the standard Activities of Daily Living (ADLs) such as dressing, bathing, eating, toileting, and transferring, then they plan to hire home care. They want to stay in their homes as long as possible.

What is a retiree to do? There are ways to offset these costs:

- *Medicare.* This federally sponsored program is open to people when they reach 65, and it has recently been expanded to provide prescription drug coverage for retirees. Medicare premiums are reasonably affordable (at least in comparison to what current workers pay), but deductibles and coinsurance do apply. Medicare supplement insurance plans are also available (feel free to shop online) that cover some of the costs not covered under regular Medicare. We find that many of our retired clients have been quite pleased with the coverage provided by Medicare and Medicare supplement plans. Medicare does not, however, provide much coverage on elder care issues; and the provisions of Medicare are always subject to change.

- *Long-term care (LTC) insurance.* On the surface, LTC insurance looks like a great idea. Elder care is certainly a risk and potentially a very expensive one. In situations like these, it is advisable to transfer the risk to someone else. It's similar to purchasing insurance in the event that your house would burn down. Sure, it's not very likely, but if it happened it would be financially devastating to most families. LTC insurance works on similar principles, but there are a number of important differences.

  ▫ You are much more likely to need elder care services than to have your house burn to the ground.
  ▫ Elder care expenses are increasing much more rapidly than the general level of inflation.
  ▫ The insurance companies don't have as much experience at estimating how many people will claim policy benefits, so they have to build in some extra cushion.
  ▫ Due to a period of extraordinarily low interest rates, insurers have not been able to earn very much on the premiums you pay.

All of the factors above have resulted in a perfect storm of problems for traditional LTC insurance. The end result is that many insurers have stopped issuing new policies, those that do issue policies make it very hard to qualify for one during the underwriting process and the policies aren't affordable for most people. Even if you can afford it now, you have no guarantee that your premiums won't be raised in the future. Finally, even if you qualify and can afford it, you could still find yourself paying insurance premiums for many years and never end up needing care. In that case, you may feel that you have wasted the insurance premiums.

Does this mean you should simply do nothing and hope for the best? Not necessarily. We typically advocate two broad approaches to LTC expenses for our clients, based on their particular situation:

- *Self-insure.* Self-insuring simply means you will cover these expenses from your existing assets. Not everyone has this luxury, of course, but this is the preferred approach because it allows you to tap into assets if the need for elder care arises. Otherwise, the assets are left intact for a surviving spouse or as an inheritance for children.

- *Self-Insure with Wealth Replacement.* Basically, you plan to keep your money invested and growing for retirement. If in the unlikely case you face a large expense related to long-term care, you will pay for this out of your retirement assets. With this strategy you purchase a life insurance policy to replace the assets potentially lost to LTC expenses. And if long-term care expenses never occur, then the surviving spouse or heirs have extra money available to support their ongoing needs. Remember your original goal—you wanted to purchase long-term care insurance in order to preserve some wealth should you require expensive assisted living. Life insurance is an interesting tool here because, whether or not you need nursing care, you are guaranteed to die someday. When you die, your surviving spouse or heirs receive a lump sum that could either be used to replace money lost to long-term care costs or to simply provide some extra financial security.

Elder care expenses are a significant risk. We have found that the best way to deal with these expenses is to focus on building a retirement nest egg that can cover these potential expenses. *Power of 5 Investing* can help you get there.

## TAX RISK

Taxes matter in retirement. The goal is to withdraw funds from the portfolio at the lowest possible tax cost *over time*. Tax laws change frequently and can change significantly over time. What makes sense in today's environment may not make sense later. When you look at the historical figures, you may well conclude that this isn't such a bad tax environment after all.

We often refer to the need for tax diversification. This means it can be helpful to locate your retirement assets in accounts that have different tax treatment. Many retirees these days have a substantial portion of their retirement dollars in what are called "qualified plans." IRAs, 401(k)s, and 403(b)s are examples of account types that fall into this category. The key characteristic of these accounts is that the assets within them have generally never been taxed during the accumulation phase and will be taxed as ordinary income when you make withdrawals. The other major category is referred to as "nonqualified." These accounts are subject to current taxation depending on the type of cash flow they generate, but much of the taxation of these assets occurs under the capital gains tax rules.

Historically speaking, long-term capital gains taxes have generally been lower than ordinary income taxes. This means there may be opportunities to exert some control over how you are taxed in retirement. If tax laws change and favor one type of account over another, then you can adjust your withdrawals to help minimize taxes. Of course, everyone's situation is different, so we recommend working with a tax expert who is well versed on the nuances of retiree taxation.

As important as taxes are, we often see people put tax minimization first to the detriment of their portfolio. For example, you have large capital gains built up in a stock you own in a nonqualified account. The stock now makes up 15 percent of your portfolio (violation of Principle Number Four), but you can't bear to sell any of it because you don't want to pay the taxes. The real risk here isn't taxes, it's the risk that the stock will take a tumble and your gains will be wiped out. Better to pay the tax and keep the portfolio properly diversified. Don't let the tax tail wag the investment dog.

Retirees should also be aware of a couple of false tax "rules" out there:

- *Always spend down your taxable (i.e. nonqualified) accounts first.* This rule of thumb has been around so long that I even hear other advisors preaching it. The thinking here is that you want your tax-favored accounts like IRAs to grow as long as possible without taxes. That's just silly. If a retiree has $15,000 per year of personal exemptions and other deductions built into their tax return, we regularly tell them to take enough IRA distribution each year to at least use up those exemptions and deductions. It's like getting a tax-free withdrawal from your IRA. Any withdrawal needs above and beyond that might be covered by withdrawals from a taxable account.

- *Everyone should have Roth IRAs!* Don't buy the hype about Roth IRAs. Yes, it would be nice if all of our retirement monies could be withdrawn tax-free. The major problem with Roth IRAs is that some people make too much money to make Roth contributions. For those who can make Roth contributions, the limits on how much you can contribute are so low that you can't really accumulate any sizable retirement account with them. The reality for most people is that the bulk of their retirement savings will occur in employer-sponsored plans like 401(k)s and their own personal savings in a taxable account. Much of the mania around Roth IRAs today is due to Roth *conversions*. In this case, you take an existing IRA and convert it into a tax-free Roth IRA bucket. Great! Except there is one catch. You have to pay all of the taxes upfront! The same taxes that would otherwise not be owed until many years from now when you take a distribution from your IRA. Paying all the taxes upfront is incredibly expensive and may even boost you into a higher income tax bracket than you would normally be in. Furthermore, you need to have the dollars available somewhere else in order to pay that upfront tax. If you have to raid the IRA to cover the taxes, you are then making the upfront tax problem even worse and may even face an additional 10 percent IRS penalty for a premature withdrawal. Finally, and this is the biggest mistake we see, the Roth conversion strategy implicitly assumes that tax rates will be higher in the future than they are now. In our experience with working with many retirees, we find this assumption to be completely wrong. Instead we often see that our clients' effective tax rates are *lower* in retirement than they are when working. Why would you choose to take the tax hit on the conversion when your tax rates are high? Just so you can feel good about having a tax-free bucket of money? That's crazy.

In the end, we think it's best to consult with a qualified CPA or an experienced tax preparer who has seen it all before. Everyone's situation is different and may require specialized help. Make sure your tax situation is integrated with your investment plan.

## LONGEVITY RISK

Congratulations! After many years of hard work and diligent savings, you have retired with a sizable nest egg. You and your financial advisor have determined that you have enough money to enjoy a comfortable retirement lifestyle, and you have developed a written investment plan to keep you on track. You're in great health. No worries, right?

Then a friend asks, "Aren't you afraid of outliving your money?"

Two generations ago, the notion of outliving one's money was laughable. Many people were elated to have lived long enough to start collecting a Social Security check. According to HumanProgress.org, a person born in the West in the year 2000 has a life expectancy of 75 years, compared to only 45 years for those born in 1900. That's an extra 30 years to accommodate in your planning. The advances in medicine, technology, hygiene, nutrition, sanitation, education, and more have combined to extend human lives far beyond what our grandparents could have imagined, and our life spans probably will get longer still. We are truly living in amazing times.

So the risk of outliving our money is very real and potentially scary. Insurance companies are even looking to cash in on this fear by offering a new tool called longevity insurance. In a nutshell, you make a large onetime payment or series of payments, say around retirement age, and the insurance company promises to start sending you checks should you reach a predetermined age like 80 or 85. Are these kinds of arrangements vital to your retirement security? Not if you have a plan.

Remember that inflation risk is the primary threat to retirees. Longevity risk is really just a special case of inflation risk. If you maintain a reasonable withdrawal rate (Principle Number Two), keep an appropriate amount of opportunities for growth in your portfolio (Principle Number Three), and don't panic during the inevitable market corrections (Principle Number Five), then living too long shouldn't be a concern for you. *Power of 5 Investing* has your back. Now get out there and enjoy those extra years!

## BONUS RISK! THE BIGGEST RISK OF ALL—DENIAL

We occasionally meet with people who just don't get it. They tell us they have worked hard all their lives, and now that they are retired, they are entitled to spend freely. A boat, a motorcycle, a new truck, a lavish wedding for a child, a swimming pool, a helping hand for the adult child who can't find a job, a vacation home, etc. They often cannot distinguish between wants and needs.

We explain *Power of 5 Investing* to them and point out areas of concern with their plan. We tell them what they *need* to hear, not what they *want* to hear. I can see it in their eyes when they have decided that we are incompetent fools—or completely pessimistic—to be warning them of such things.

Here's what we share with them:

- Failing to plan is planning to fail.
- You need a plan, and you need to take action.

There is no government bailout for individual retirees. Either you take responsibility for your financial future, or you live on whatever Social Security pays you. Your choice.

If they're in denial, they are running the biggest risk of all. Unless they face up to all the other threats and recognize what they can do to their retirement dreams, they cannot overcome them. Such was the case with the retired widow who converted her stocks to cash and missed the recovery. She had not acknowledged what inflation would do to her. Without a plan in place, dollars dwindle and dreams fade.

As the old saying goes, "Denial ain't just a river in Egypt." If you've read this far and find your wants exceeding the limits outlined in *Power of 5 Investing*, perhaps it is time to reconsider your options.

Retirees face many significant risks, but they can be overcome. The timeless principles of *Power of 5 Investing* were specifically developed to navigate the risks and guide you to a comfortable retirement. You can persevere and prosper with *Power of 5 Investing*.

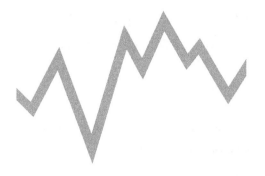

# CHAPTER 8

## IS IT TIME FOR A PARTNER?

You don't *need* a financial planner. But you might *want* one.

I honestly believe the above statement, and I've told people that many times. There are people out there today doing their own planning, managing their own investments, and getting along just fine.

After all, who knows you better than you know yourself? You can maintain full control and knowledge over what you own. There's no conflict of interest. Best of all, the annual fee that is commonly charged for financial planning services stays in your pocket.

As a do-it-yourselfer, you will still need some help. The following resources are ones that I have found personally valuable over the years and are regularly cited for their consumer friendliness. Where appropriate, I have included references to specific resources. While not a complete list, the sources here should come in handy:

- Estate Planning

  - Deborah Jacobs, *Estate Planning Smarts*
  - Alexander Bove, Jr., *The Complete Book of Wills, Estates & Trusts*
  - Alexandra Armstrong & Mary Donahue, *On Your Own*

- Investing

  - Jeremy Siegel, *Stocks for the Long Run*
  - Moshe Milevsky, *Are You a Stock or a Bond?*
  - Nick Murray, *Simple Wealth, Inevitable Wealth*
  - Morningstar.com
  - Anything written by John Bogle
  - Benjamin Graham, *The Intelligent Investor*

- Taxes

  - Ed Slott, *The Retirement Savings Time Bomb*
  - Natalie Choate, *Life and Death Planning for Retirement Benefits*

- Economics & History

  - Thomas Sowell, *Basic Economics*
  - Peter Bernstein, *Against the Gods*
  - Niall Ferguson, *The Ascent of Money*
  - John Steele Gordon, *An Empire of Wealth*
  - Michael Kelly (of JP Morgan Chase), *Guide to the Markets*
  - Brian Wesbury, *It's Not as Bad as You Think*

You will notice that the list above does not include any specific recommendations for online retirement calculators or apps. Partly this is because the technology is constantly changing, usually for the better. There are also countless variations in the assumptions and models used underneath all of these tools, which can lead to sometimes conflicting answers. Try out several of the best known ones, understand the underlying assumptions being used in each, and use them all as approximations.

Whichever tools and resources you use, be sure to write down your plan and revisit it at least annually. Measure your progress against your goals, hold yourself accountable, and stick to the plan.

## THE COST OF INVESTOR BEHAVIOR

We've already determined that people can do their own financial planning, and some do it quite successfully. So you're smart and focused. You've done all the research. You've documented your financial goals, put a plan in place to achieve them, and you're ready to go.

Many others have gone before you. How have they done?

Since 1994, DALBAR, Inc. has issued its annual *Quantitative Analysis of Investor Behavior*. In it's most recent 2014 edition, the data and the conclusions have been nearly the same as in prior years. Some data:

- For the latest 30-year period ended December 31, 2013, the average stock mutual fund investor earned only 3.7

percent annually, while the S&P 500 earned 11.1 percent annually. That is a huge gap of 7.4 percent per year.

- What are the sources of this gap? About 1 percent is due to poor mutual fund selection. Another 1 percent or so is due to fees and expenses of investing in mutual funds. The rest is attributable to emotions and lack of discipline. Retail mutual fund investors have shown a consistent pattern of piling into funds that recently had the best performance, followed by bailing out of those same funds when their ranking falls or returns are less than expected or there is a hiccup in the market. This buy high, sell low approach regularly dooms retail investors.

Even worse:

- The DALBAR report concludes that attempts to correct irrational investor behavior through education have proved to be futile. The belief that investors will make prudent decisions after education and disclosure has been totally discredited. Instead of teaching, financial professionals should look to implement practices that influence the investor's focus and expectations in ways that lead to more prudent investment decisions.

- Similarly, Louis S. Harvey, president of DALBAR, argues, "It is now past the time for the investment community and its regulators to understand that the principle of educating uninterested investors about the complexities of investing is unproductive... We need a fundamental change that transforms investment thinking into meaningful decisions and choices for retail investors."

## THE VALUE OF A COACH

The DALBAR study has two key takeaways:

1. *Investors need a plan.* That plan needs to be informed by research and expertise. *Power of 5 Investing* can be that plan.

2. *Investors need discipline.* Discipline allows them to stick with the plan through good times and bad. They can get that from themselves or from us.

These two points illustrate why clients work with us.

- They *hire* us because we have a plan (takeaway number one). We have spent years acquiring the training and experience, and we have distilled this into *Power of 5 Investing*. Plus, let's face it. Finance is pretty boring stuff unless you're a self-professed finance geek like me. I'm really not very interesting.

- They *keep* us because we provide the ongoing discipline (takeaway number two). And also because we're nice people.

I've had clients call me their financial shrink and their investment coach. The coach analogy is an interesting one because, when I look at my own life, I use coaches all the time.

My doctor is a coach. Look, I love steak and ice cream. I know I'm better off eating fish and fruit, but the other things are just so delicious! My doctor recently did some blood work, analyzed how various foods I eat may be leading to health issues caused by inflammation, shared the results with me, and recommended some changes that are making a real difference in how I feel. I still eat steak and ice cream but not as often. My doctor (medical coach) created a plan and is helping me monitor it. Having to go back and see her is leading to discipline and accountability.

My trainer is a coach. I recently had a shoulder injury from a sports accident. I was out of shape, coupled with general wear and tear on my body from playing competitive sports far longer than I was qualified to do so, and I simply overdid it. I also am "allergic" to gyms and exercise machines, so working out has not been an option. I was referred to a trainer (health coach) to rehab my shoulder. He developed a routine to strengthen my shoulder and made me do the rehab work with him in the gym. And I actually paid him for this! That's discipline.

My backpacking instructor is a coach. I live in Colorado and love the outdoors. Skiing, hiking, hunting—anything to be out in the sunshine and fresh air. But doing those things the wrong way in Colorado can—quite simply—get you killed. So I enrolled in a class to learn backcountry survival skills. The class was six months long and included a textbook, homework, hands-on learning, and tests. My backpacking instructors (survival coaches) had a plan, and they expected me to learn what is in the lesson plan and then demonstrate to them in a series of wilderness excursions that I have mastered the skills. The discipline comes fairly easily here; either do what they say or you will find yourself lost, cold, hungry, and alone in the wilderness.

Coaches provide a plan and instill a true sense of discipline. If you can provide your own plan and discipline when it comes to your retirement security, good for you. We find that most people benefit from a financial coach.

## HOW TO CHOOSE A FINANCIAL ADVISOR

Do you enjoy keeping up with financial markets and tax changes? Do you see other full-time professionals for expert guidance, such as doctors, lawyers, and tax specialists? Do you prefer face-to-face service, or are you satisfied with calling an 800 number? These are personal decisions that only you can make.

If after looking into these matters, you decide that you want a financial planner after all, here are some things to consider. In choosing a financial advisor, you need to insist on quality. You can start by getting referrals from trusted sources, such as professional organizations. Good resources include the Financial Planning Association (Fpanet.org) and the Certified Financial Planner Board of Standards (Cfp.net). Always check the credentials of your prospective advisor. You can find information on the Securities & Exchange

Commission website (Sec.gov) and at the BrokerCheck site of the Financial Industry Regulatory Authority (Finra.org).

When you do meet with an advisor to assess whether you want a relationship, these are some of the questions you should keep in mind:

- What is your process?
- What are your qualifications and experience?
- Do you specialize in clients who are similar to me?
- With whom will I be working?
- Is comprehensive financial planning included?
- How are you paid?
- Are you limited in which financial products you can recommend or use?
- If there is a situation in which my interests and yours might not align, will you tell me about this in writing?

At the end of the day, trust your gut. There should be a personal connection with your advisor. You need someone you feel comfortable being totally honest with. If that very personal level of comfort isn't there, you haven't found the right advisor for you.

## ASK THOSE WHO HAVE GONE BEFORE YOU

We asked members of our Client Advisory Board what advice they would give prospective retirees. In their own words, here are a few of their comments:

- "You don't know what you don't know."
- "I'd rather set my nose hairs on fire than invest on my own."
- "2008–2009 taught us a lot."
- "I already left the working world. Why would I want to go back to work managing my money?"
- "I want to spend my time *generating memories.*"

One gains perspective over time about what really matters. A decade into retirement, many of our clients tell us that time spent with loved ones has been much better than time spent watching the markets.

## YOUR PARTNER—OXFORD FINANCIAL PARTNERS

Oxford Financial Partners has been leveraging its time-tested approach to financial planning for decades. We believe it is our privilege to help our clients articulate their financial goals and then work with them to put plans and programs in place to help ensure they are on a path to fulfill those goals. We provide independent, objective financial planning and investment advice to our clients. As representatives of a national SEC Registered Investment Advisory firm, we are able to provide independent, objective financial planning and investment advice to our clients. Clients have told us that we are their "financial doctor"—a description we love to hear, as it is indicative of the close relationships we value and the way we think about their short- and long-term financial situation.

Our clients range from those who are just starting to think about and plan for retirement to those who are in retirement and want to ensure their funds are sufficient—and their long-term wishes intact. No matter where you are in your retirement journey, we can partner with you to help assess where you are and work with you to make your goals a reality.

## THE PARTNERING PROCESS℠

We have found over the years that laying out a clear process for serving our clients yields tremendous benefits. We call our approach The Partnering Process because it reflects the long-term partnership approach we take in assisting clients.

Oxford Financial Partners created The Partnering Process to help us collaborate with you better and to assist you in achieving your financial goals. The Partnering Process follows a systematic approach to delivering personalized financial planning and investment advice to our clients.

The Partnering Process consists of three phases.

1. *Planning.* Generally three to four weeks from time of initial meeting, which culminates with delivery of The Financial Wellcheck (see next page).

2. *Implementation.* Generally completed within eight weeks of your initial meeting.

3. *Reviews.* We conduct annual reviews on a planned basis; we will also meet with you whenever you have questions or your circumstances warrant reexamination of your portfolio. In addition, you receive monthly and quarterly statements with information on your account. Finally, your total financial picture is available online through the Personal Financial Portal, 24 hours a day, 7 days a week, 365 days a year.

The Financial Wellcheck is a proprietary tool that provides our clients with a road map they can follow on the way to achieving their financial goals. We present The Financial Wellcheck to you at the end of the initial planning phase. From there you may choose to retain us to implement the recommendations and continuously monitor and report on your progress over time, or you are free to implement the recommendations on your own.

# THE FINANCIAL WELLCHECK<sup>SM</sup>

Client: Joe & Jane Smith
Date: July 2014

| FINANCIAL AREA | CRITICAL COMPONENTS | | NEXT STEPS |
|---|---|---|---|
| **Estate Planning** | | | |
| a) Estate Documents | Will, Living Will, Power of Attorney, Health Care Proxy, Trusts (2008 - Attorney name here) | | |
| **b) Beneficiary Designation** | IRA 1: Primary: Joe 100%; Contingent: Fred 50%, Mary 50% | | |
| | IRA 2: Primary: Joe 100%; Contingent: Not listed | **STOP** | Need Contingent |
| **Risk Management** | | | |
| a) Life Insurance | **Lincoln Life, $1,500,000 death benefit, owned by trust** | | Continue Funding |
| b) Long Term Care | N/A - Discussed at 2009 meeting; determined that coverage too expensive | | |
| c) Disability Income | N/A (retired) | | |
| **Retirement/Education Planning** | | | |
| a) Retirement Progress | Current / 3-year withdrawal rates: 5.1% / 4.9% | | |
| b) Employee Stock Options | See attached analysis | **CAUTION** | |
| c) Education Planning | Education goals achieved **Assumed $25,000/yr. tuition, 5% inflation, $250/mo. contribution, 6.7% growth** | | Continue Funding |
| **Cash Flow Management** | | | |
| a) Distributions and Taxes | **Current Monthly Cash flow** | | |
| | Jane IRA Distribution | $5,000 | |
| | Less 20% federal / 5% state taxes | ($1,250) | |
| | **Net deposit to client** | **$3,750** | |
| b) Required Minimum Distribution | **$55,357 for 2014; satisfied by monthly distributions ($60,000)** | | |
| c) Tax Reduction Strategies | Capital gains tax avoided of $8,698 from PG sales made in 2013 | | |
| **Investment Management Strategies** | | | |
| a) Goals Documented | Investment Policy Statement dated 3/15/13 | | |
| b) Portfolio Returns | Lifetime Return (1996): Deposits $2,000,000; Withdrawals $1,000,000; Current $2,550,000 | | |
| | Three year average annual return (after fees and expenses): 8.2% | | |
| c) Power of 5 Investing® | 5% withdrawal rate | | |
| | 5 years stability bucket | | |
| | **5% diversification limit: Client desires 10% PG position** | **CAUTION** | |
| d) Portfolio Rebalancing | See attached proposal | **CAUTION** | Joe & Jane sign proposal |

We do not charge anything for the planning phase. We find that charging for this step can become a barrier to the client taking the time to get started with their planning. We're willing to make the investment of our time and expertise into your financial success. We find this goodwill gesture gets the relationship off to the right start and often leads to the person becoming a long-term client.

The decision about whether to hire a financial advisor is a challenging one. I find that most people would like to have this burden taken from them, but knowing who to trust creates real hesitation, even fear. This is all perfectly understandable. At Oxford Financial Partners we've tried to make the process as open and nonthreatening as possible. Do some realistic soul searching about your desire to handle your finances, ask friends and trusted advisors who they recommend, interview several advisors, then make the decision that feels right to you.

Whether you choose to use an advisor or not, be sure to follow the powerful principles found in *Power of 5 Investing*. Your retirement portfolio will thank you!

# AFTERWORD

## THIS BUSINESS OF LIVING WELL

One of the many blessings in my life has been to find myself doing work that exposes me to so many wonderful people. I wake up each day knowing that, in serving others, I have the opportunity to make a meaningful difference in other people's lives. The trust and confidence that our clients place in us is both humbling and gratifying.

Clients often tell us how much they appreciate all that we have done for them, how we have helped them plan for a secure retirement, enjoy a special vacation, or help with a grandchild's education. But instead of them thanking us, it should really be the other way around. When retired clients tell me how they got to where they are today, and what they still hope to achieve, I am continuously amazed. I don't think they realize how much wisdom is being conveyed in the stories they tell and the life experiences they share. Our clients are sharing the wisdom of a life well lived, and I'm always making mental notes.

Some of the greatest wisdom ever imparted to me by a client came, ironically, when I attended his funeral. It was, without a doubt, one of the most amazing celebrations of a person's life I have ever seen. Everyone who attended his service shared some stories, some laughs, and some tears. I always knew he was a very special person, but I don't think I truly understood just how deep his passions ran when it came to helping others. I remember thinking if I end up touching half as many lives as he did, it will have been a pretty good life. It truly was inspiring.

In his book *Enough*. John Bogle shares his own observations on this wisdom of the ages:

"*Financial wealth*, in fact, is a shallow measure of success. If we accept dollars as our standard, then 'money is the measure of the man,' and what could be more foolish than that? So how *should* wealth be measured? What about a life well lived? What about a family closely bound by love? Who could be wealthier than a man or woman whose calling provides benefits to mankind, or to his fellow citizens, or to her community or neighborhood?"

I have some clients who are twice my age, and it is my privilege to tap into their storehouse of experiences and wisdom gained through the years. I, too, learn and grow from our relationship and from their perspective on what truly matters in life. I am pleased to be able to advise them on financial matters—but I can testify that they have advised me on life. Money is just a tool. Each of us must find a way to use it effectively as we go about this business of living well.

In my relatively short time on this earth, I've packed in quite a few life experiences. Most of them great, a few not so good, but all of them valuable. I still believe that tomorrow will be better, no matter what obstacles we face. I also know that life can be short, and there are no guarantees. As Andy Dufresne says in *The Shawshank Redemption:* "I guess it comes down to a simple choice, really. Get busy living, or get busy dying."

To those who have shaped me over the years, and to those who continue to impact me, I offer my sincerest gratitude. *Thank you!* It is a true privilege to work with so many wonderful people. I look forward to serving you all for many years to come.

*Oxford Financial Partners is truly honored and blessed to have been a part of so many families' lives over the years. We now proudly serve clients in more than 20 states across the country. If you like what you've read in this book and are interested in working with us, please contact us. Any financial topic you wish to cover is on the table; the agenda is yours.*

## As always, this session is complimentary.

*8050 Hosbrook Road*

*Suite 200*

*Cincinnati, OH 45236*

*Phone: 513.469.7014*

*Fax: 513.672.0363*

*Toll Free: 866.469.7014*

## Staff@OxfordFP.com

Printed in the USA
CPSIA information can be obtained
at www.ICGtesting.com
JSHW012039140824
68134JS00033B/3155

9 781599 325385